Doughboy's Diary

by
C. Earl Baker

 Burd Street Press

This Burd Street Press publication
was printed by
Beidel Printing House, Inc.
63 West Burd Street
Shippensburg, PA 17257-0152 USA

In respect for the scholarship contained herein, the acid-free paper used in this book meets the guidelines for permanence and durability of the Committee on Production Guidelines for Book Longevity of the Council on Library Resources.

For a complete list of available publications
please write
Burd Street Press
Division of White Mane Publishing Company, Inc.
P.O. Box 152
Shippensburg, PA 17257-0152 USA

Library of Congress Cataloging-in-Publication Data

Baker, C. Earl (Chester Earl), b. 1893.
    Doughboy's diary / by C. Earl Baker.
        p.   cm.
    ISBN 1-57249-100-0 (acid-free paper)
    1. Baker, C. Earl (Chester Earl), b. 1893--Diaries. 2. World War, 1914-1918--Campaigns--France. 3. World War, 1914-1918--Personal narratives, American. 4. United States. Army--Biography. 5. Soldiers--United States--Diaries.   I. Title.
    D548.B28 1998
    940.4' 8173--dc21   97-48924
                                                             CIP

PRINTED IN THE UNITED STATES OF AMERICA

For all the men of the American Expeditionary Force (AEF)

CONTENTS

ILLUSTRATIONS

FOREWORD

On June 28, 1914, in Sarajevo, Bosnia, a Serbian nationalist, Gavrilo Princip, shot Francis Ferdinand, Archduke of Austria, and his wife, Countess Sophie Chotek, and plunged the world into World War I. The assassination sparked the powder keg which years of convoluted alliances by closely-related rulers had made of Europe.

Nearly every Western power was involved, one way or another, the Serbian countries on Germany's south, the Russians on their Eastern front and, on the Western front, France, the Netherlands and England.

Even when the Germans' deadly submarines brought down the Lusitania and other ships carrying Americans, President Woodrow Wilson maintained America's neutrality, though he worked night and day to negotiate peace with the Central Powers, as Germany and her allies were soon called. The Germans had developed a deadly new weapon, which they named "Big Bertha", a huge, long-barreled gun, capable of dropping giant-sized shells on Paris from a distance of fifty miles. The powerful war machine aided Germany's eventual overrunning all Europe. The depredations of the Central Powers outraged humanity. It seemed only a matter of time until America entered the war.

Almost like an actor waiting in the wings, Francisco "Pancho" Villa, a two-penny Mexican revolutionary rejected by his own nation, appeared on the scene. On March 9, 1916, at Germany's instigation, he crossed the border between Mexico and the United States, burned Columbia, New Mexico, and killed some of the citizens in a ploy to divert Wilson from throwing America's strength into the European war on the side of the Allies. The invasion, like nothing so much as a cockroach attacking an eagle, backfired on Germany in a big way; it gave us the perfect reason for mobilizing and training men for war, ostensibly against the laughable clown, Pancho Villa, but, ultimately, against the Central Powers in Europe.

Wilson called on John Pershing, the seasoned veteran of Indian wars and the Spanish-American War, to send Villa scuttling back across the border. The year before, Pershing's wife and three daughters had died in a fire in the family quarters at the Presidio in California, so he was suffering from great personal grief as he led American troops against Villa.

Pershing supervised the training of America's young manhood for war. From all over America, volunteer regiments converged on Texas to prepare for war.

I was one of those men who, with my comrades from Huntingdon, Pennsylvania, formed Company F of the 28th Division. As I write this in 1976, I am 86 years old and obsessed with telling what I remember of my fallen comrades before I, too, "go west."

PREFACE

My father, Chester Earl Baker, author of *Doughboy's Diary*, was born on December 15, 1893. After the war, he returned to the printing trade, sometimes writing an account of the battlefield amputation performed by Jimmy Bottomfield, and another of the night the sentinel/chaplain prevented Company F from marching into certain death, which were published in the VFW magazine.

In 1921, he married Maximilla Heck. They had five children, four girls and a boy. All his life, he "mother-henned" his buddies, keeping an unofficial roster of Company F, recording when each old comrade "went west." He joined them on January 22, 1980, at which time, to the best of his knowledge, only two other Company F veterans remained alive.

After his death, along with his manuscript, we found a poem he'd written after attending one of his buddy's funeral. I think there can be no more fitting ending to my father's story.

Millie Baker Ragosta

CHAPTER 1

Enlistment

In the spring of 1916, like every other young man of Huntingdon County, Pennsylvania, I followed the war news eagerly. Though President Woodrow Wilson had been trying desperately to get the warring European powers to sit down together to negotiate a peace, his pleas for sanity fell on deaf ears. Indeed, Germany's aggression seemed certain to pull America into the war soon.

At twenty-two, having learned the printing trade at the *Daily New Era* Publishing Company, where I'd been employed for nearly eight years, I was busting for a change. My desire to help the war effort gave me the excuse I needed. I left the printing company to help make munitions at the newly-opened Mount Union Powder plant, which was always short of manpower. Explosions and escaping sulphuric acid made working in the plant nearly as hazardous as fighting in Europe. Nevertheless, the pay was great and, like all young fellows, I figured I was invulnerable. Besides, America would need all the munitions she could get when we entered the war.

When Pancho Villa's raid gave the United States a gold-engraved invitation to prepare for war, Company F, 8th Regiment, 7th Division of the Pennsylvania National Guard, quickly mobilized in the armory at the head of Seventh Street in Huntingdon. Full company strength was 150. At the time of Villa's raid, it was a mere 75, so a vigorous recruitment campaign began; squads went all over Huntingdon and into the surrounding towns, appealing for recruits.

I needed no urging to join. Fighting a war was a whole lot more glamorous than making munitions for it. Honesty compels me to admit that the enthusiasm of Huntingdon County's young women for soldiers in uniform had at least as much to do with my decision to join the army as patriotism. I suspect the very same reason influenced more than one County young man, for our ranks rapidly swelled to 123 recruits, all champing at the bit to lick Pancho Villa, after which we'd take on the Kaiser.

To us recruits, that spring of 1916, playing at soldiering was something of a lark. We drilled on the old athletic field at the south side of the Fourth Street bridge and went for long hikes along Stone Creek, under the benign command of First Lieutenant Harry E. Robb, a much-loved school teacher who'd taught some of us at the William Smith school. Commanding officer though he was, we called him Uncle Harry as a mark of our love and respect.

When we had leave, proudly clad in ill-fitting and badly worn National Guard dress blues, we dated hometown girls. To us—and to the girls—the shabby blue uniforms seemed mighty sharp in contrast to the khaki field uniforms with leggings, leftovers from the Spanish-American War, which we wore for training.

The armory became home to those soldiers who lived away from town; members who lived in the town of Huntingdon were permitted to sleep at their homes when not on guard duty. Guarding Huntingdon County's railroad tunnel and bridges as well as several factories was vital since all were quite feasible targets for sabotage. Indeed, so important were they considered that a company of state militia from Philadelphia arrived in Huntingdon to guard the town, establishing a tent city on the field below Huntingdon along Stone Creek. The arrival of these city fellows occasioned many a fight as the Philadelphians rivaled hometown boys in vying for local girls.

We entrained for El Paso, Texas on July 7, 1916, stopping at Mt. Gretna, the Spanish-American War training camp at Indiantown Gap, Pennsylvania, where we were given physicals. Then it was back onto the crowded trains for a trip halfway across the country.

We arrived at a stretch of desert—future home of Camp Stewart, five miles north of Fort Bliss, Texas—the second week of July. To Pennsylvania boys, used to lush green woods and meadows, Texas seemed an outpost of hell. The train disgorged us at a siding where the only sign of human habitation was a huge standpipe capping an artesian well. Thirsty, we drank from it, finding the water warm and unappetizing. We looked at each other and then around the barren waste of cacti and sage, wondering what we'd gotten ourselves into. Many voiced their opinion of the guy who'd chosen this God-forsaken spot for an army camp. And we soon learned that we, whose only training had been hiking in long-familiar woods, performing the manual of arms, and learning to clean our 1905 Springfield rifles, were expected to build an army camp for the constantly arriving troops.

However, we set to it. As we toiled in the unaccustomed 110 degree heat, one of the boys erected a sign identifying us as The Pennsylvania Land Improvement Company. We dug latrines, pitched 8-man tents over lumber floors of our own construction, installed little iron Sibley stoves in each tent, and avoided the ever-present rattlesnakes; we scratched sand-fleas, ate tinned salmon, stewed tomatoes and weak coffee, and cussed out our sergeant, Nick Musgrave. Even gentle old Uncle Harry Robb came in for his share of abuse by one disgruntled recruit.

"I think that old son-of-a-bitch lays awake at night, thinkin' up more stuff to torment me," he groused after taps one night.

There was a flurry of protest from those of us who knew Lieutenant Robb better.

"He's a smart man who knows more about the history of warfare than you'll ever know, buddy," I said. "Just remember what he told you: 'There are only two kinds of soldiers in a war, the quick and the dead.'"

"He's tough on us because he wants us to stay alive," said another defender. "To do that, we've got to toughen up."

"If he don't kill us first," came back the sour reply.

I must admit that, in the beginning, I was every bit as convinced that Sergeant Musgrave had it in for me as my grousing tent mate was that Uncle Harry hated him. Indeed, not long after we arrived on the desert, I protested to Sergeant Musgrave about what I saw as too many guard-duty assignments.

He glared at me from under his hat brim. "Baker, it's not my fault your name begins with a B. We only got 123 recruits. Now get the hell outa' here till I blow my whistle for roll call."

That exchange convinced me complaining did a fellow no good in the army; in fact, my guard-duty assignments increased. Moreover, when two other recruits—my cousin, James "Chesty" Smith, and Chal "Baldy" Rittenhouse—also complained, he set the three of us to loading wheelbarrows with sand, pushing the barrows fifty yards into the desert, dumping the sand, and going back for more. After several hours of this, needless to say, our bellyaching stopped.

It wasn't all back-breaking toil, however. For entertainment, we played cards, arranged boxing matches and impromptu talent shows, and held endless bull sessions. Once, thanks to a violinist named Vincent, we staged a hilarious square dance. On passes to Fort Bliss or El Paso, we ogled the Texas girls, took pictures of each other walking on the backs of three aged and lazy alligators basking in the sun beside their pool in the El Paso park, and bought California wine at 35 cents a gallon.

Enlisted men were paid $16 a month, part of which was withheld to send home or for Liberty Bonds, giving us the enormous sum of about $11 a month to spend. Not surprisingly, the camp was soon a hotbed of amateur entrepreneurs. Those who could sketch, drew comic pictures of soldiers wearing baggy uniforms in hair-raising predicaments with rattlesnakes and tarantulas. These sketches were then taken to an El Paso engraver who made a plate and ran off a thousand or so cards which the enterprising artist would peddle up and down the streets of the five-mile long encampment. There were also card sharks and chuck-a-luck games for the very naive.

Two of the Company F boys were not from Huntingdon County. Hugh Little and his buddy, Chick Strange, who had been bumming around the country on freight trains, chanced to stop off in Huntingdon during the Company F recruiting drive. They quickly joined up. We promptly dubbed Hugh, who was a veritable giant, Big Hugh Little. Hugh was accustomed to making a living wherever he chanced to land. He soon developed a lucrative taxidermy business, capturing and stuffing hundreds of the little horny toads that infested the desert. They looked like nothing so much as miniature prehistoric monsters. He'd give samples to his friends who sold dozens of them, mostly to officers, for one to five dollars each.

Like soldiers everywhere, relieving the ever-present boredom and outwitting "the brass" became the major leisure activity. On one such occasion, Chesty, Baldy, and I slipped over the border illegally to see the famous statue of the Virgin Mary, "Our Lady of Guadeloupe." Since no American in military uniform was permitted to cross the International Bridge at El Paso, we had to wade the Rio Grande to get into Mexico.

We made a game out of eluding Mexican military observation as we climbed the peak above the city of Juarez for a closer look at the magnificent statue. Just as we started our descent in the dark, we almost fell over a Mexican soldier, lolling at the base of the statue, an empty bottle beside him. Quickly retreating back up the slope, we couldn't resist tormenting the obviously drunk guard by rolling big stones down the steep slope toward him. At first, he looked startled, then, evidently deciding that if he ignored the intrusion, it would go away, he stared stoically in front of him, pretending to be oblivious of the bigger and bigger boulders we rolled down the hill. Only the arrival of the sentry's relief—who, we reasoned, might not yet be inebriated at the beginning of his turn at guard duty and, so, shoot at trespassers—put a stop to our game and sent us moving furtively down the mountain, listening for the inevitable rattlesnakes, and across the river to camp.

Since we'd missed evening roll call and were not even in our bunks at taps, we were punished severely for our adventure . . . guard duty for a solid month and the distasteful chore of emptying the big nighttime urinal. This was a can placed in the middle of the company street for the convenience of guys who had to urinate in the middle of the night and didn't want to go clear to the latrines. Considering the rattlers and sidewinders a sleepy man might encounter in the dark, using the can was a prudent course.

Inevitably, there were men who figured out ways to avoid duty. One of these was Jim Kurtz, a runt with a perpetual quid of tobacco in his cheek, who created an ingenious method to get out of hard work. He would carry a bottle of strong smelling liniment in his pocket and any time he saw the approach of a sergeant with work duty in his eye, he'd slip behind a tent and apply the liniment freely to his neck, then, adjusting his head to what appeared to be a painful angle and contorting his face, he would shuffle hesitantly into view. The sergeant would take one look at the "suffering" man and find another soldier for the chore he had in mind. Not surprisingly, the malingering recruit soon earned the nickname of "Liniment Jim." During our service in Texas, I never once saw him wielding a pick or shovel, though he was almost always in any party going to El Paso to take in a movie. He was as inseparable from his bottle of liniment as from his sack of Union Workman tobacco.

However, later, during the company's physicals at Camp Hancock, Georgia, as the American Expeditionary Force (AEF) prepared to go to France, Jim scorned using his gold-bricking device. He was a brave soldier, wounded in one of the AEF's first engagements in France. Ironically, a piece of shrapnel no bigger than a kernel of grain went completely through his neck in the very spot where he'd rubbed liniment to avoid cleaning latrines.

We all had our nicknames on the border. Bill Holder dubbed me Zebediah—don't ask me why—which soon became shortened to "Zeb." I'm 86 at this writing and the other two Company F men yet alive *still* call me Zeb.

One of the Company F men I most admired was Sergeant Ernest Cutshall. He drilled us until we, too, were experts in the care and use of our Springfield 30 calibre rifles. Not only was he one of the best shots in the company and an authority on guns, but one of the bravest and most gentlemanly men I ever knew.

Ernest was standing by me one day as I received a pass to go to El Paso. "Would you like some company, Private Baker?" he asked.

Pleased at this attention from my idol, I said, "Gosh, yes, Sarge," and fell into step beside him.

In El Paso, we visited several hardware stores and hock-shops, looking for Sarge's passion: guns for sale. To his delight, he found and bought a little honey of a 32 special lever-action Carbine. Later, as we passed a saloon, still smiling over his purchase, he asked me if I'd like a beer. His pay wasn't all that much more than mine and, knowing his reputation for insisting on buying drinks for his companions, I declined.

However, just then, the bat-wing doors of the saloon flew open and a big Texas ranger landed on the sidewalk. Seconds later, a second ranger came through the door and landed neatly beside the first. As we gazed down at them in astonishment, Sergeant Nick Musgrave, my old nemesis, came out of the saloon and ran off around the corner. The fallen rangers, bellowing with fury, jumped to their feet and followed.

Sergeant Cutshall and I exchanged startled glances and took off after them, but Nick had disappeared, leaving the Texans, rubbing various aching spots and muttering soft, Southern curses.

Curious to see what had happened, we went into the saloon where Nick's friends were whooping with delight.

"What happened?" Sergeant Cutshall asked.

"Those Texas boys started makin' disparaging remarks about National Guardsmen in general and Northern National Guardsmen in particular, so Nick taught 'em some manners," one of them explained.

My opinion of Sergeant Musgrave improved immensely.

When we returned to camp, Nick was standing in the opening of his tent, the roll call book in his somewhat battered hands.

"Nice goin', Sarge," I said.

"You saw that show, Baker?"

"Only the finish. But the fellows who saw it all said the beginning and middle were spectacular."

He lowered his voice. "You'll forget what you saw unless you want to be emptyin' the piss can until hell freezes over."

So much for admiring *that* sergeant. "Sure Sarge, won't say a word."

He looked down at the roll call book, his face impassive. "Then get out of here, Private," he barked.

I did.

By now, Cavalry Colonel "Black Jack" Pershing's presence on the border had driven Pancho Villa into the mountains and there was little chance Company F would ever get to engage him. We'd always known, of course, that the expedition to Texas was to train troops for the war in France but we'd all been secretly hoping for a chance to pursue the penny-ante Mexican bandit. Though President Wilson was still trying to keep America out of the war, Germany's aggression on the seas with the great fleet of submarines they'd built had already killed a number of American citizens, riling the nation. Wilson's efforts to get Germany to talk peace, admirable as they were in theory, had come to nothing.

In any case, as the weeks of desert living with its boiling days and frigid nights—without once catching a glimpse of Pancho Villa—wore on, the main topic of conversation was when we'd be going home. One cold night, as Christmas drew near, Jim "Foxy" Lewis, who was considerably older than the rest of us, came into our tent to borrow a chaw of tobacco from Jim Kurtz. Foxy settled down and began to chew contentedly, occasionally spitting a stream of tobacco juice toward the stove which caused a hissing, fragrant steam to fill the tent.

"What d'you think, Foxy?" Liniment Jim asked. "Will we be goin' home by Christmas?"

Foxy stared at the stove contemplatively and let another stream fly. "You yard birds ain't *never* goin' home."

Liniment Jim threw a big lump of coal at him, driving him back to his own tent.

We didn't make it by Christmas. But the company cooks did their very best to make the day as much like what we would have had at home as possible. They labored all day on the twenty-fourth of December, cleaning and stuffing turkeys, baking pumpkin and mince pies, peeling bushels of potatoes. They decorated the mess hall with what evergreen and twisted crepe paper they could scrounge, and spread nuts, oranges and candy out on an improvised counter at the end of the big dining hall. Company F drew the first watch and, to a man, during the long hours of guard duty, anticipated the feast to come.

Toward evening, a well-fed Company G came to relieve us. We'd just lined up at the head of our company street for roll call, preparatory to eating the long-anticipated Christmas dinner, when one of those damned Texas desert storms came out of nowhere. Gale force winds drove sand into every nook and cranny of the vast, crudely-constructed camp.

Though the storm blew itself out quickly, our Christmas dinner was ruined, except for the nuts, oranges and whatever candy was still in wrappers. Needless to say, we were the most demoralized bunch of yard birds in Texas that night.

But, at last, on February 20, 1917, we mustered for the train ride home. Every one of us swore he never wanted to see Texas again. A pet lover all my life, I had captured and tamed a little prairie dog I called Billie. I'd bought him a collar and chain and let him ride on my pack as we marched to the train. However, true to military maneuvers everywhere, it was hurry up and wait; once we arrived at the tracks, we sat for over an hour in a strong north wind before the train rolled onto the siding.

Before daylight, we'd been told that no one was to leave the group, but, when we were ordered to fall in for roll call before boarding, one man, Private Chal Hawn—commonly known among the men as "Old Colonel" or "Puss"—was missing. No one could answer Captain Charles H. Hatfield's questions as to his whereabouts. The Captain looked grim as he ordered us onto the train and we all hung out the windows, watching for Private Hawn, afraid he'd be left behind, perhaps, charged with being AWOL. At the last minute, the six-foot tall, perpetually hungry Puss moseyed into view, munching on a chocolate pie. Captain Hatfield grinned in spite of himself and a cheer went up from the men as they pulled him onto the train. Bored with the long wait to entrain, Puss had slipped through the chaparral at the south end of the camp for a last forage for food before leaving Texas.

We arrived in Huntingdon on February 24, 1917, toughened by our sojourn in the desert. Some of us, myself included, were the proud possessers of an expert rifleman's rating.

Billie managed the journey home but, to my sorrow, succumbed to Pennsylvania rats the following week when he tried to dig a hole to hibernate in a field behind the house.

Knowing our careers as private citizens would be brief, I tried to talk Jim Kurtz—who'd been working at the Westinghouse plant in East Pittsburgh—into joining me at the nearby munitions plant.

"Much better money, Jim," I said. "And you'll be close at hand when the call comes to muster again."

"Well, won't hurt to take a look," he agreed and rode the daily shuttle train to Mount Union with me one morning. But it took a very small look, indeed, before Jim declared he wanted nothing to do with making munitions, however eager he was to use them.

"Come to Pittsburgh with me, Zeb," he urged. "You can get a job operating a punch press and you won't have to worry about getting your head blown off in a damned munitions plant."

"I don't know anything about punch presses."

"That's okay. I'll teach you on the trip out. Just tell the personnel man that you have lots of experience. Say you used to work over at their Swissvale Plant," he counseled.

So, off we went to East Pittsburgh to work for Westinghouse until the muster call sounded, leaving our addresses with Captain Hatfield. My bluff about knowing how to operate a punch press worked and, soon, I really did know how.

We hadn't long to wait for the muster; one evening, a few weeks after our return from Texas, when we reached the Turtle Creek boardinghouse where we lodged, I found that the landlady had shoved Captain Hatfield's night letter under my bedroom door. I opened it and read, "Report to the Armory, Tuesday morning, 8:00 AM for muster. Tell Kurtz. Signed, Captain Hatfield."

We were going to get ready for the real war.

CHAPTER 2

Off to War: England

The old armory at the head of Seventh Street once again became home to the boys of Company F. Lieutenant Robb led us on long hikes and drilled us with rifles and in military marching. The Philadelphia boys were still camping on the field along Stone Creek at the eastern end of Huntingdon and they had better than half a year to make time with our girls while we were in Texas.

On April 6, 1917, the United States declared war on Germany and our drilling took on a new urgency. The following May 18, the Selective Service Law was passed. Undermanned National Guard units then received men from Camp Lee, Virginia, from North and South Carolina, and from other army camps throughout the states. Some of Company F's recruits had received discharges upon our return from Texas due to age, infirmity or personal responsibility, reducing our number considerably. But our uniform-clad soldiers launched another intensive recruiting drive and soon brought us up to wartime strength of 150, with enough local volunteers to fill our quota.

The reorganization left me with only one member of my original squad, my old pie-eating comrade, Puss Hawn. Besides Puss, the newly assigned squad members were Bill Bagley, Frank Bagshaw, Preston Brown, Wilbur Corbin, Bill Edwards, and Frank Homman.

In September, the boys of Company F climbed aboard a train bound for Camp Hancock, Georgia, which had been a training camp during the Spanish-American War. Almost everyone in town turned out to bid us farewell. The Red Cross and Salvation Army supplied us with box lunches, freezers full of ice cream, oranges and candy, tobacco, and cigarettes.

One of our men, Bruce Honstine, over the vigorous protests of his doctor, demanded to be discharged from the hospital where he'd been admitted with typhoid fever, likely first contracted in Texas. Pale and shaky, he climbed aboard the train with the rest of us. However, he was soon ordered back home. When we learned he had died in the J. C. Blair hospital, we considered him our first non-combat casualty.

We arrived at Camp Hancock, a wilderness of sand and jack pine near Augusta, Georgia, during the night of September 10, 1917. The War Department ordered the Huntingdon company—Company F of the 8th Regiment—combined with Company F of the 16th Regiment, largely boys from northwestern Pennsylvania, forming a new Company F, henceforth of the 112th Regiment, 28th Pennsylvania Red Keystone Division.

The red keystone, until now, the identification symbol of the Pennsylvania National Guard, was to be worn on all clothing and painted on the steel helmets of all Pennsylvania soldiers. A further distinction of the new Company F was that of being the red shock division, always the first to begin an attack. And I was now a corporal.

One result of the reorganization of our company was not so welcome. For the first time, Huntingdon County boys were separated. Some of our number were sent to other—machine-gun—regiments, specifically, the 107th, 108th, and 109th. Company F was then brought up to strength by draftees from Camp Travis, Meade, and Lee, so though we were largely a company of volunteers, we were no longer exclusively so.

To our sorrow, we lost Captain Hatfield who was given command of a Pioneer Infantry Battalion and went overseas with them. Also, Major George B. Corbin, First Lieutenant Harry E. Robb, and Second Lieutenant William M. Corbin were honorably discharged, either because of their age or medical condition. This broke Lieutenant Robb's heart; he wouldn't be going overseas with "his boys." As he bade us good-bye, his eyes were damp and his shoulders drooped. He was to live a long time in civilian life, tenderly teaching many a child of his Company F comrades. Until he was an aged man, he was a great favorite of Huntingdon's children—his beloved little pupils—who vied with each other for the privilege of holding his hand as he led large groups of them on field trips around town.

At Camp Hancock, the new 112th Regiment and other units of the 28th Division reprised their Camp Stewart experience by literally building the camp from the ground up for the recruits who would follow. The first chore was clearing trees and cutting them into firewood, burning the stumps and leveling a huge parade ground for drilling. We built an enormous recreation building which housed the library, cafeteria, and game room big enough for showing movies. We also built a chapel for holding religious services for all denominations, a canteen where candy, writing paper and such could be purchased, and stables for the officers' horses.

After years of conventional, open-field combat, the Europeans had begun fighting from trenches and so would we. So, in a big, old dry reservoir, we dug a trench system, complete with communicating trenches, dugouts, and firing bayous, calculated to familiarize the rookie soldiers with this new phenomenon. Lieutenant Joseph A. Landry, of the Army Corps of

Engineers, and Captain Ryan, a British bayonet specialist, instructed us. Soon, we were leaping from trenches, racing across open areas, and thrusting our bayonets at targets we'd constructed . . . hanging, man-sized bundles of the brush we'd cleared to build our training ground. Every soldier, under Captain Ryan's tutelage, became proficient in the use of the bayonet. When his tour of duty at Hancock ended, Captain Ryan remarked, "The 28th Division will go overseas, second to none, in the use of the bayonet."

With the new Eddystone rifles we'd been issued, Company F consistently scored high on simulated combat drills where targets popped up from pits, much as in amusement park shooting galleries. Once, because we Pennsylvania country boys shot so rapidly, a team of "regular" army scorers thoroughly reprimanded us for firing without aiming. But to their astonishment, when they checked our targets, our score of hits was the highest ever recorded. We attributed the excellent scores as much to our years of hunting rabbits back home as to our practice in Texas, where many of us had already earned one expert rifleman badge. We were just as proud of the second ones earned at Camp Hancock.

In addition to acquiring rifle and machine-gun proficiency, we mastered the throwing of hand grenades while jumping a trench. Our instructors urged us to imagine the trenches filled with German soldiers.

We also had to master the usage and handling of a one-pounder cannon. The gun was equipped with rifle sights and mounted on wheels. To fire it, you had to lie on the ground behind it; otherwise, the recoil action could kill you. On the march, a small donkey pulled the gun. However, the United States had a way to go to catch up on artillery, so much of our training was in the use of the French Chauchat rifle, an 8mm light machine gun. Each infantry company was equipped with one and a French soldier was attached to the camp to instruct us in its use. One of our huskiest men, Bob Appleby, was chosen from our company to use the French rifle, not only because of his proficiency with it, but because the gun, with its three ungainly legs, was heavy and required a fairly muscular man to lug it on long marches. We also trained with the British 55mm long-range cannon whose range was exceeded only by Germany's Big Bertha.

Each company also had a trench mortar, a hollow tube, six inches in diameter, that could be lowered or elevated, depending on the target, to toss the heavier grenades.

Even though an infantryman was not likely to be assigned to a trench mortar or a machine gun, everyone was required to become proficient in operating all artillery since, in battle, if the man operating a weapon was killed, the nearest man might have to take over.

In the spring of 1918, we were ready to go overseas. The word finally came at evening roll call on April 24. The next day, the full regiment paraded through the streets of Augusta, proudly joined by a few feeble ex-Confederate soldiers in their tattered uniforms, on the way to the trains that would carry us to Camp Upton, New York.

Our commander, Captain David Sutherland, had graduated from West Point. However, he was promoted out of the unit and Lieutenant Joseph P. Connell, formerly of the old 16th Regiment, was assigned to command the company. Our new lieutenants were James Ross Thompson and Philip Burdick.

All along the way from Georgia to New York, enthusiastic crowds jammed every railway station. At Washington and Philadelphia, Red Cross ladies and representatives of other organizations served us the best refreshments they could devise.

At Camp Upton, our overseas gear was brought up to date and we were given further physicals. In addition to my leadership of a rifle grenade squad, I received the post of Company Gas NCO which involved the responsibility of issuing, inspecting, and attaching new filters to the gas masks we were issued as well as setting up and manning gas signal alarms when the Germans hit us with phosgene, chlorine, lachrymose or mustard gas. While phosgene and chlorine were the most deadly, lachrymose—or tear gas—was the most troublesome. Mustard gas burned blisters all over the body, but, now that the Allies had figured out methods of treating it, it was seldom fatal as phosgene gas and chlorine gas often were. I was the oldest child of a big family which may explain why I'd already gotten the reputation of being something of a mother hen. I guess the company officers figured they could count on me worrying about my friends inhaling gas and so, would fulfill my duties well.

The evening before we sailed for France, Sergeant Ernest Cutshall and I were cleaning our rifles in the barracks assigned to us when a big sergeant from another company came stumbling into the room, obviously somewhat inebriated.

"Either you boys got any liquor?" he asked.

We hadn't and told him so. He glared at Sergeant Cutshall.

"I never liked you," he said, and picking up Sergeant Cutshall's hat from the bed, jammed it down on Ernest's head.

Though he easily outweighed the gentle Sergeant Cutshall by twenty pounds, before the drunken sergeant knew what hit him, Ernest had grabbed him by one arm and, with a quick twist of his hip, tossed the big oaf over his head. The surprised sergeant, stretched out breathless on the floor for several minutes as Ernest returned to cleaning his rifle, soon staggered to his feet and left the room.

A few minutes later, another sergeant stuck his head in the door and looked around.

"Not another one," Sergeant Cutshall sighed.

But the newcomer wasn't looking for trouble. "Where is everyone?" he asked. "You two the only ones here?"

"Just us," Ernest said cheerfully, polishing the barrel of his rifle.

The sergeant came into the room and threw a beautiful fountain pen on the bed beside Sergeant Cutshall. "Either one o' you guys wanna' buy a nice pen for a buck?" he asked.

Ernest looked at it and declined. I picked it up. The pen had vine-like gold filigree encircling a mottled brown barrel.

"Biggest dollar's worth you'll ever see, Corporal," the sergeant urged.

"I can see that. It's worth more. Why do you want to sell it?"

"I need a drink."

Now, I'm as venal as the next man but I didn't want to profit from another soldier like that. I took a dollar from my pocket and, wrapping it around the pen, handed it to him. "Consider the dollar a loan."

He put the dollar into his pants pocket, then, leaning over, shoved the pen into my shirt pocket. "It's yours. I don't want it." I felt bad about getting it for such a small price but I really couldn't afford more.

"It's a valuable pen. You'll be sorry," I said. "I told you, you can pay me back later—"

"I don't want the damned pen. It was given to me as a going-away gift when we went to Hancock by a girl I was engaged to. At first, she wrote me every day. Then the letters stopped coming and she wouldn't answer mine."

I nodded, understanding his wanting to get rid of the pen.

"The other boys in my company knew what was happening but they didn't like to tell me," he went on dolefully. "I found out when someone sent me a copy of my hometown paper with her engagement to a damned slacker in it."

"That's tough luck," Ernie said.

The sergeant turned and left the room, throwing a final remark over his shoulder as he went. "I don't want to see her or the damned pen again."

Sadly, he didn't. He was killed on Le Chene Tondu ridge during the Argonne Forest battle. As for me, the jilted sergeant's sad face always came back to me when I used the pen and I was glad to trade it to another soldier later on.

On May 7, at Pier 59 in New York City, 9,000 Pennsylvania soldiers, including our 112th Regiment, marched up the gangplank of ships bound for England. Company F was lucky enough to draw a British cruise ship, one of the Cunard line, called the *Aquitania*, which had been hastily adapted as a troop carrier.

The *Aquitania* was manned by English naval officers and men, some of them disabled from active combat but still doing their bit for the war effort. Just before the big liner put out to sea, to our disappointment, all soldiers were ordered below decks. Probably just as well that we didn't have to gaze on the Statue of Liberty until she disappeared from our sight; we were feeling emotional enough as it was.

Because the *Aquitania* could out-run any submarine, we sailed without the usual destroyer escort. On the trip across the Atlantic, we did sight one submarine and sank it. Every day of our crossing was bright and sunny and khaki-clad soldiers stood thick at the rails all through the voyage. I imagined any German subs watching for us would have thought the ship had been camouflaged with khaki blankets. It was during the crossing that the 28th Division began to be designated the Keystone Division from our red emblems.

We landed at Liverpool on May 14 and marched down the gangplank to the excited shouts of the English, who, physically and emotionally exhausted after several years of war, were delighted to have our help. One grizzled soldier with a wooden leg, watching from the sidelines, yelled, "When you get up front, give 'em 'ell, Yanks."

We marched to a railroad siding where trains waited to carry us across England to Dover, on the Channel. When we reached the train shed and were permitted to drop our heavy packs, we were soon surrounded by smiling girls and women, handing out donuts, cocoa . . . even flowers. Nothing was too good for the men who had come to the relief of their husbands, dads, and sweethearts.

A train loaded with British soldiers—Tommys—heading back to the front after being hospitalized for battle wounds, rolled slowly past our waiting train. From every window, men leaned out to shout exuberant messages to us. "We'll be seeing you up the line, Yanks; give 'em bloody 'ell." "Welcome aboard, Yanks." "Glad to 'ave you with us."

One decidedly Scottish voice shouted, "What's goin' on here, Lassies? How about *us* blokes? Don't we get any o' the bloody stuff?"

A pretty, laughing English girl shouted back, "Hold your bloody tongue, Scotty; you'll get your share. It's only polite to serve these American boys first; they've come to help you."

We thanked the ladies of the canteen committee, then climbed aboard the little train for the trip to Dover. The automobiles and locomotives we saw from the train windows looked like toys to us compared with our enormous engines back home. However, despite the hard wooden seats, we enjoyed looking at the beautiful countryside as long as daylight lasted.

As morning dawned, the outskirts of London shimmered, pale and indistinct, through the chilly fog which permeated the very railroad cars. By now, the wooden seats, lined along each side of the troop train, had become torture, along with our empty stomachs and dirty bodies. As we passed through Canterbury, we got a good look at the beautiful cathedral.

We left the train at Folkstone and marched through the high iron gate of a large rest camp there. When the last of us had entered, we suddenly became aware of our proximity to "The Great War" when the gate was locked behind us. The worn and stained uniforms of the camp personnel showed the effects of several years of war. However, brass belt buckles and buttons were shined to a fare-thee-well, as if in defiance of the shortage of fabric.

The kitchen crew fed us: an inch-square piece of cheese, a hard bun with a meagre dab of marmalade and a cup of weak tea. British rations, like their uniforms, were a stark reminder of the years of bitter struggle. I'm afraid we Yanks, used to the plentiful food at our training camps back home, didn't yet understand that the Brits were giving us all they had to give. I heard one of the kitchen personnel ask his mate, "What d'you think of this, Jock? When I handed that red-headed bloke a bun, blimey if he didn't take *two*!"

The ungrateful—and hungry—Yank stared mournfully at the tea and said, "I'd give my last dollar for a cup o' Java and a piece of my mother's apple pie."

As we ate this simple meal, the English soldiers regaled us with tales of action at the front and gave us much advice about surviving trench warfare for, by now, the trenches were the principal battleground of the war.

At last, Lieutenant James R. Thompson called, "Fall in, men." Eager to be on our way, each of us grabbed his pack and moved into line for the long march to Dover.

At this point, we found that we wouldn't be making the 22-mile crossing until the following day. The entire 2nd Battalion was billeted in an old apartment house of some kind, with a view of Dover Castle, overlooking the Channel. "Hey, boys, that castle sits right atop the white cliffs of Dover," Bob Appleby yelled enthusiastically from his post by the narrow window. "Come take a look."

His suggestion was met by curses as the weary soldiers flopped down on the dusty, splintery floor without even bothering to unroll their blankets. Those that didn't fall instantly asleep added curses for their officers, the British and each other. Mercifully, they didn't realize that a bare floor in an old English building would seem like the softest bed at the Ritz compared with the rat-infested trenches we were soon to be sharing with "seam squirrels" or "cooties" as the doughboys came to call the ubiquitous body lice.

When we had rested, we were issued passes to visit the town, where we brought welcome business to the grocery stores and shops.

On May 16, we finally marched to the seaside where we packed ourselves like sardines aboard the transport, *Onward*. With a squadron of British destroyers and battle planes, we set out on the choppy sea.

We were going to France.

Most of us had crossed the Atlantic Ocean without suffering unduly from seasickness; I can't say the same for the 22-mile Channel crossing. The flimsy little boats dipped alarmingly on the choppy waters. Low-flying fighter planes guarded our passage from above and speedy destroyers escorted us through the water like strong mother hens herding flocks of fat peeps. The destroyers roiled up more tempestuous waves for our queasy stomachs to deal with, but we were mighty grateful for their protection all the same. The German submarines and bombing dirigibles had made a nightmare of the Channel.

At last, we landed at Calais. Bob Appleby looked around and grinned. "Baker," he said, "do you realize that just sixteen days ago, we were still in the good old USA?"

It was hard indeed to realize that.

We shouldered our packs and hiked to Rest Camp 6 which was nothing more than a tent city on a sea of black sand. To our dismay, we learned that we were to be absorbed into the British army for combat training.

The next day, we marched to a large army depot and, to our bitter disappointment, were ordered to turn in our uniforms, gas masks and Eddystone rifles which were to be stored for the duration of our training. It was a bleak feeling to pack our own uniforms into large barracks bags, then don British uniforms—some bloodstained—whose last owners had been battle casualties. We hated surrendering our accurate Eddystones for the short-barrelled Lee-Enfield rifles of the English army—likewise reclaimed from the battlefield and so, often inaccurate—and the Tommies' worn and patched gas masks. The British officers explained that our better equipment would be here, waiting for us, when we finished our weeks of training.

Food supplies were alarmingly low. On top of that, the Allies had the care and feeding of many German and Turkish prisoners of war at Rest Camp 6. Therefore, perpetual crowding and hunger became our lot. Tents made for 8 men had to accommodate 16. Each tent was positioned over and around a four-foot deep hole, into which, at the first sound of air raid sirens, we were to jump and lie on our backs, feet toward the center pole, our steel helmets over our faces.

We hadn't long to wait for our first war experience. Just before dark, two days after landing on French soil, German bombers were heard overhead. A faint buzzing, like nothing so much as a swarm of tormented bees, grew louder and louder, sounding like a fast locomotive across the heavens. Then the high-flying bombers began releasing their cargos which exploded like giant firecrackers on the small, but strategic town of Calais.

"To the tents, Yanks," our British instructors yelled and we raced for cover. However, some of us, not wanting to miss our first sight of combat, stayed out of the pits to watch the show. Searchlights threw pencils of light into the twilight as antiaircraft guns tried to get a sight on the planes. As night drew on, the fury of our first air raid baptized us new soldiers thoroughly.

As I lay on the sand, watching the air show, I felt a small tin can in the sand, perhaps lost by a picnicker, heaven knows how long before. By the sporadic light, I opened what proved to be a can of small sausages. Being a young man with a hearty appetite which had been unsatisfied since we landed in England, I opened the can and sampled a sausage. I should have known better. What resulted from my impromptu snack was my first—but by no means my last—experience with the dysentery we soon learned to call the G.I.s. Most of us were to have recurring bouts of it for the rest of our days.

We underwent a period of intensive training in the use of gas masks, trench warfare, and close combat which included bayonet drill, grousing all the while about training under English instructors. However, they did have the firsthand experience that American officers couldn't boast and, somehow, despite the inaccurate training rifles, we earned our musketry proficiency certificates.

We couldn't wait until we were serving under our own officers, wearing our own uniforms and carrying our own rifles— American fighting men at last.

We assured each other that, now that we had arrived, the war would surely go better for the Allies.

CAPTAIN CHARLES H. HATFIELD, COMPANY F

FIRST LIEUTENANT HARRY E. ROBB, COMPANY F

C. E. Baker Collection

SECOND LIEUTENANT WILLIAM M. CORBIN, COMPANY F

C. E. Baker Collection

COMPANY F RECRUITS DRILLING ON SOUTH FOURTH STREET DRILL FIELD, HUNTINGDON, PENNSYLVANIA. PINEY RIDGE AND OLD DISTILLERY IN THE BACKGROUND

C. E. Baker

MEMORIAL DAY PARADE, 1916, HUNTINGDON, PENNSYLVANIA, NOTE CIVIL WAR VETERAN, SECOND FROM RIGHT

C. E. Baker

MAN ON RIGHT, CARL "POOGEY" COFFMAN, BLAIR PARK, 1916

C. E. Baker

SKETCH OF INTERNATIONAL BRIDGE BETWEEN
EL PASO, TEXAS AND JUAREZ, MEXICO, 1916

Sketch by C. Earl Baker

PAYDAY FOR COMPANY F, 1916, HUNTINGDON, PENNSYLVANIA

C. E. Baker

"THE PENNSYLVANIA LAND IMPROVEMENT COMPANY,"
CAMP STEWART, TEXAS, 1916

C. E. Baker

COMPANY F MOUNTAIN CLIMBERS, 1916, IN MEXICO. <u>LEFT TO RIGHT</u>:
"LINIMENT JIM" KURTZ, ARTHUR GERLACH WITH CLUB FOR RATTLERS, BILL
"JAY BIRD" HOLDER, AND AUTHOR

C. E. Baker Collection

C. BAKER (AUTHOR) AND PRAIRIE DOG, BILLIE, CAMP STEWART, TEXAS

C. E. Baker Collection

AUTHOR DOING LAUNDRY, CAMP STEWART, TEXAS

C. E. Baker Collection

DAVID PRICE, "CHESTY" SMITH, MULE SKINNER, "RED" GRAY, AND
AUTHOR WITH THE VIOLIN HE COULDN'T PLAY WORTH A HOOT

CAMP STEWART TRIO:
DAVID PRICE, AUTHOR, AND "CHESTY" SMITH

FRONT ROW: BILL EDWARDS, JIMMIE WHITE, PRESTON BROWN, HARRY "MAD IKE" MAIER, AND CHARLES "RED" GRAY. BACK ROW: HARRY D. FIGARD, CARL ANDERSON, WILBUR CORBIN, JOSEPH GATES, AND BRUCE HONSTINE

C. E. Baker

C. EARL BAKER, CAMP STEWART, TEXAS

Hazel Baker Parks

HUNTINGDON CITIZENS SEEING COMPANY F OFF FOR EMBARKATION
POINT, 1917. MAN IN SLOUCH HAT, WITH FACE PARTIALLY OBSCURED
IN RIGHT FOREGROUND, IS AUTHOR'S FATHER, GEORGE BAKER; LADY IN
SUNBONNET, HIS MOTHER, NORA.

C. E. Baker

VIEW OF CAMP HANCOCK, TAKEN FROM THE GEORGIA-BOUND
TRAIN, ROUNDING A CURVE NEAR WINSTON-SALEM, NORTH CAROLINA

C. E. Baker

FALL-OUT TIME AT CAMP HANCOCK

C. E. Baker

COMPANY F COLUMN, CAMP HANCOCK. LAST
TWO MEN ARE FIRST LIEUTENANT HARRY ROBB AND
SERGEANT ERNEST CUTSHALL.

C. E. Baker

COMPANY F RESTING,
CAMP HANCOCK, GEORGIA

C. E. Baker

MESS LINE AND KITCHEN TENT, CAMP HANCOCK

C. E. Baker

FRANK HOMMAN, CAMP HANCOCK. THE FIRST SOLDIER FROM HUNTINGDON KILLED IN COMBAT. THE LOCAL AMERICAN LEGION POST IS NAMED FOR HIM.

C. E. Baker

CARL ANDERSON, CAMP HANCOCK

C. E. Baker

JAMES "SNAKEY" WILSON, BUGLER, CAMP HANCOCK

C. E. Baker

"SNAKEY" WILSON, BUGLER, CAMP HANCOCK

C. E. Baker

BILL EDWARDS, AUTHOR, AND BILL BAGLEY, 1917, CAMP HANCOCK

C. E. Baker Collection

JOHN PRICE, SMUSHY LIGHTNER, AND "DUTCH"
SHIRM, COOKS, CAMP HANCOCK

C. E. Baker

HOMER HECK, CAMP HANCOCK

C. E. Baker

CHAL RITTENHOUSE AND
HARRY "HUT" LUCAS, CAMP HANCOCK

C. E. Baker

AUTHOR IN TREE, CAMP HANCOCK

44

LEFT TO RIGHT: COOK, "DUTCH" SHIRM, CHAL RITTENHOUSE,
DAVIS MCEWEN, AND "SCHOOLTEACH" PRICE, CAMP HANCOCK

C. E. Baker

PORTRAIT OF AUTHOR TAKEN AT AUX-LES-BAINS, FRANCE, 1918

C. E. Baker Collection

COMPANY F, 8TH REGIMENT, PENNSYLVANIA NATIONAL GUARD AT CAMP STEWART, TEXAS, IN 1916

C. E. Baker Collection

COMPANY F, IN HUNTINGDON IN 1917, AFTER BEING RECRUITED
TO WAR STRENGTH BEFORE GOING TO CAMP HANCOCK, GEORGIA

C. E. Baker Collection

CHAPTER 3

France: Trenches and Gas Warfare

On Sunday morning, May 19, shouldering our 70-pound packs and belts full of ammunition, we finally left Rest Camp 6 and marched to the Fontinette station on the other side of Calais. According to our British instructors, Rest Camp 6 was a "blighty" place, which, close as we could figure, meant it was a haven of rest. At the time, we laughed at the notion. Shortly, we would look back with longing to our "blighty" beds at Rest Camp 6.

We boarded the railway cars marked, "hommes 40, chevaux 8." After the war, these boxcars became famous because veterans formed an organization called Forty-and-eight, open to any soldier who'd ridden in the boxcars. They were, truly, jammed with 40 men and more, though I can't say we had 8 horses to share our dirty, crowded, one-day-and-one-night ride. Our rations, issued before we entrained, were a few hardtack biscuits and two cans of corned beef. We passed through St. Omer, thirty miles from Calais, and on to Lumbres where we detrained. Needless to say, we were delighted to alight from the filthy boxcars and begin a two-day hike to several villages—Bayenghem, Seninghem, and Waterdal—behind the Flanders front. Company F drew Seninghem.

Long before we reached our destination, we were cursing the guy who'd ordered wool uniforms with summer coming on. Later, after we'd had our own uniforms—winter issue—restored, we realized that, since we hadn't the option of *both* summer and winter wear, the woolen cold-weather garments were absolutely vital to the predominantly damp, cool days of northern France.

We were billeted in barns and cow-byres scattered throughout the small villages. The luckiest of us pitched tents under the ever-present, leafy apple trees.

Many of the Flemish farm folk had never seen an American, but they welcomed us enthusiastically. They had suffered even more than the English since 1914 and rejoiced that we'd come to help.

48

I confess, we Company F boys, coming from a conservative little town where babies were "brought in the doctor's bag," were somewhat disconcerted by the French peasant's earthy approach to life, the entire village making an eagerly-watched spectacle out of the mating of their mares and stallions. To our amazement, both sexes openly urinated in public and heaps of reeking cow dung stood in front of every door. But the people, God bless them, were friendly. They shared with us from their meagre stores and came to the concerts the 112th band organized on Sunday afternoons.

Most of the villagers were either children or very old adults. Certainly, there were no young men in the village, all being away at war or already killed, and only one young woman. She was, perhaps, sixteen and might have been pretty had she ever cleaned herself up enough to tell. All the time we were billeted in her village, she wore the same dirty garment over which her greasy, yellow hair spilled down. She was hardly a doughboy's dream mademoiselle. Even so, one soldier, more desperate for feminine companionship than the rest, tried to get acquainted with her. She giggled, and, shaking her head, said, "Americain soldat, non bon."

"Nuts to you, too, mademoiselle," replied the disgruntled soldier and promptly dubbed the poor girl, "The Cowshit Queen."

We were ordered to continue training in the area until summoned to the front. This consisted of six-mile hikes each day to a hillside drill field where we practiced throwing dummy hand grenades and listened to lectures. Several times, we hiked to Lumbres for rifle-range practice with the hated English Lee-Enfields. The Company F boys, so many of whom had taken expert rifleman badges back home with our Eddystones, now failed miserably. The inside bore of mine was so worn it looked like a shotgun; I finally complained to our Tommy instructor.

"Let me try it, Yank," he said.

He took several shots at the target, missing more widely than I had. Grinning apologetically, he handed it back to me. "Well, it'll get a Jerry at 100 yards."

I fervently hoped he was right. In any case, I did earn a certificate: "Number 2 Brigade School-Musketry Course-A group. Corporal C.E. Baker, F Company, 2nd Battalion, 112th Regiment, U.S.A.

Knowledge of rifle: very good

Work during course: excellent

Remarks: good instructor

Signed, Major A.H. Catchole."

On Memorial Day, General Pershing visited the 28th Division's training area. Earlier, when he'd first seen American boys in British uniforms, drilling with British arms, he'd protested to President Wilson, threatening to resign if the practice didn't stop at once. The president promptly gave him all authority as supreme commander of the army. The practice of British officers giving last minute combat training when the American companies arrived in France did continue for a short time.

However, soon after Pershing's inspection, the 28th Division received orders to exchange the borrowed uniforms and equipment for their own. And, a few days later, instead of heading into battle with the Brits, we prepared to march as *American* troops.

We left Seningham, Bayengham, and Waterdal on Sunday, June 7, for the march to the front. As we marched southeast, the column moved parallel to the British line near Arras, always within sound of the guns. After three days hard marching, sleeping in barns and sheds at night, we reached a town called Wavrans, where we camped.

The American Expeditionary Force, after further training, was to join the British troops deployed along the Marne River. The German High Command had poured all its might into a great offensive in which Chateau-Thierry was the bull's-eye of its target. In a desperate bid to win the war before the AEF could swing the tide in the Allies favor, the Fifth German Offensive had pushed to within 25 miles of Paris.

One old mule skinner called Scotty, survivor of the British Checkerboard Division which had been nearly annihilated at the battle of Kemmel, and whose uniforms and transports we'd been issued, became so attached to Company F that he applied for a transfer to the American army.

"The blighters turned me down, Yanks," he said as he bade us a sad good-bye.

It was at about this time that Captain Sutherland was ordered to the army general staff and Lieutenant Harry McCluskey was given command of F company for a brief time. But, to our satisfaction, it soon went to the much-loved Lieutenant James R. Thompson, who was to hold it until the end of the war.

On the evening of June 9, we returned to the trains; we were on the move again. For the most part, though, for the next few days, we hiked, the longest and most grueling marching we'd yet endured. Occasionally, for a short while, we got a chance to ride a while on the French "Pullmans" for men and mules. Somewhere, I picked up a French map and was able to trace our route. We reached a village called Tremblay on June 14, where regimental headquarters had been established in an old chateau. We could see the Eiffel Tower on the skyline.

We were billeted in a large, clean barn and, each day for a week, drilled in the open fields nearby. We were given leave to visit the village in the evenings where we tried to parlez-vous with any French girl who would listen to our awkward attempts to speak French. We had been strictly cautioned not to fraternize with any women or girls, but the admonition was honored only in the breach. To ask homesick soldiers not to try to communicate with the pretty village girls was tantamount to setting a dish of meat scraps before a starving pup and forbidding him to eat.

Since we were now to be attached to the French Fifth Army, regimental orders came down to prepare for an inspection by the French General Muire and his officers along with our own Colonel Rickards on June 17. Despite the primitive conditions at our camp, we did our best to bring ourselves and our gear up to army spit and polish and the warm approval of the general filled us with pride.

In Tremblay, we also got our first payday since landing in France. As long as our money lasted, the shopkeepers did a thriving business. They had to compete with the army card sharks, however. One boy I knew sent $5,000 home to his folks, having easily trounced doughboys who didn't know an ace from a deuce.

However, some of us, Puss Hawn, Sergeant Ernest Cutshall, Oscar "Awkie" Beck or "Boy" as his best friend Puss was wont to call him, Jimmy White and myself were not about to blow our whole pay in the village when Paris was so close. So, one evening, stopping at the local estaminet for some bottled refreshments to take along, we set out for Paris.

Jimmy White was a member of Headquarters Company, playing the flute in the 112th Regimental Band and he didn't drink hard liquor. He was a loyal and true friend and, till the day I die, I will be ashamed of the dirty trick Puss Hawn and I played on him.

Deciding the champagne Jimmy *would* taste was not strong enough to get him enjoyably drunk, Puss and I filled an empty bottle with whiskey, champagne and red wine. We told Jimmy the estaminet-keeper said it was the closest thing the French had to red soda pop.

"It won't even give you a decent buzz," I lied.

The trusting Jimmy tasted it.

"Pretty good, is it, Jim?" Puss asked.

"Not bad. Not bad at all," the poor fellow answered. And, as we swaggered on toward Paris, getting drunker by the minute, Jimmy kept up with us, swallow for swallow, out of his "red soda-pop" bottle.

We reached the wide boulevard leading to Paris. By this time, our arms—not to mention the rest of us—were looped and we were singing at the top of our lungs, "The mademoiselle from Armentiers, parlez-vous, she hasn't been kissed for years 'n' years, parlez-vous . . ." when a big, black limousine pulled to the side of the road and a bunch of military police piled out.

"Where the hell do you drunken, crazy fools think you're going?" one of them—a sergeant—shouted.

"Why, to Paris," Puss said with a big grin.

"Did you hear what he said?" the sergeant thundered to his companions. "He's going to *Paris!*"

The others glared at us while the sergeant continued to cuss us out.

Finally, arms akimbo, he barked, "I'd run yez all in, but the jails of Paris are full of crazy sons-o'-bitches already, so about face and get the hell back to wherever you came from."

Sergeant Ernest Cutshall saluted him. "Yes, Sir!" he said, doing his best to sound military. "And thank you. I'll see that they get where they belong."

We started back, but, perhaps not too surprisingly, we never reached our nice, clean barn billet that night. Puss noticed a haystack and flatly refused to go another step in spite of Ernest's entreaties. Puss struggled mightily to crawl to the top of the haystack, always falling backward in the process. Finally, incredibly, he got to the top and stretched out. "More hay, boys," he kept saying, "more hay." Oscar tried to coax him down, but when all his pleadings fell on deaf ears, he said, "If you ain't goin' back to camp, I ain't either, Colonel. Gimme a hand up that haystack."

But Puss was already asleep. Awkie finally gave up trying to scale the stack and fell asleep at the base of it. We left the two of them sleeping. We'd not gone far when big Ernest stumbled over something in the dark and fell like the walls of Jericho. I obviously didn't get much farther because I woke up the next morning in a cemetery with a pounding head and barely enough time to make roll call. Puss and Awkie came stumbling in shortly.

A rumor began making the rounds that the division would leave in a few days for Chateau-Thierry where a battle was raging between United States Marines and the Germans. The ranks were filled with excitement. We'd been in constant training and had not expected to see action so soon, but the determined German advance against Paris mandated the use of every fighting man, ready or not.

On June 20, the 112th Regiment was ordered to move.

Fortunately, the YMCA truck from Paris had arrived before we left Tremblay, enabling me to buy two small notebooks. I had been recording our experiences—making my handwriting as small as possible—on every scrap of paper I could get my fingers on: envelopes from home, candy-bar wrappers, anything that would take the awful, grainy French ink in my fountain pen.

One man bought all the chocolate bars and gleefully gouged all his buddies until an officer got wise to his profiteering and stopped it. He was later seriously wounded and mustered home. Perhaps, not surprisingly, he became a politician. However, to his credit, I must say that no veteran ever asked a favor of him without receiving it.

So, we left our nice, clean barn at Tremblay and marched to various small towns near Louviers, the new site of regimental headquarters. On June 23, we were lorried 70 miles to La Tretoire near the Petit Morin River, east of Paris, by our allies, Chinese Nationalist troops, whose teeth were all black from chewing betel nuts. American doughboys chewed tobacco for the same reason the Chinese boys chewed betel nuts; it laid the dust.

As we rolled slowly through a French village, a pretty little French girl ran toward the last truck where I was sitting on the tail gate, my feet over the edge. She extended a white flower toward me. "Pour vous," she said with a shy smile.

Amid the cheers of my envious buddies, I jumped to the ground and addressed her in the few words of French I could summon. "Merci. Promenade avec moi, mademoiselle, oui?" I asked.

She threw me a dazzling smile and took my arm. As we walked along behind the lorry, she looked at the buttons on my uniform and said, "Souvenir, oui?"

I pulled a button loose and gave it to her.

"Merci, beaucoup, American soldat," she murmured.

She reached into the pocket of her apron, withdrew a photograph of a young soldier in a French uniform and handed it to me.

"Your sweetheart?" I asked.

She shook her head. "Non, non, mon frere . . . brother," she said.

That was a relief to me.

"Where did you learn the English word?"

She managed to convey she'd learned a little at school. As the trucks began to pick up speed, I said, "I must go," and made motions of jumping back on the truck.

Quickly, she took a pencil stub and a scrap of paper from her pocket and scribbled something on it.

"Fini le guerre, you return, oui?" she asked and thrust the paper toward me.

"Oui, darn tootin'," I said, running toward the truck. I saw that the scrap of paper contained her address. I stuffed it into my pocket as my drooling buddies pulled me aboard.

At last we reached Bussieres, where we were billeted in cow stables and a pigsty. Here, we picked up the lice that would be our bane till the end of the war. There was simply no way to avoid the little beasties since our lodging was inevitably on dirty straw. We thought longingly of the big, clean white barn we'd lived in at our last post as we picked the bloodsucking "cooties" from our hides. The well-initiated French soldiers told us to dip our clothing in pails of boiling water to rid them of the hellish parasites but that was, obviously, out of the question most of the time. For all practical purposes, we were stuck with the damned things until after the war when we'd all gone—twice—through the delousing mills at Le Mans. One Company F boy, Private Fred "Comrade" Flake, who always managed to lighten our moods with his clowning, used to offer to trade especially large cooties for two small ones. "Comrade" has long since "gone west"; I pray there are no big cooties to torment him now, nor little ones either.

Just as lice became a wartime reality to us, so did the continual bombardment. The battle front was now only a short distance from our bivouac. At night, we had grandstand seats for pyrotechnic displays macabrely reminiscent of July 4 celebrations back home. Except that *these* fireworks killed and maimed.

We were very close to the front now. Chateau-Thierry on the Marne lay just on the other side of the hill from where we were camped. Lieutenant Thompson, our scout and liaison officer, was extremely selective about who accompanied him on scouting missions and usually called on Private Jimmy Bottomfield. One day, when Jimmy was not available, Lieutenant Thompson picked me. Needless to say, I was deeply pleased and flattered by this mark of approval from the gallant, young officer who could laugh at danger as heartily as he laughed at accidentally sitting on a pile of excrement in the dark.

We were ordered to dig sleeping pits for the night. I had long since discarded my entrenching shovel, having more interesting stuff to carry . . . battlefield souvenirs to sell or barter to guys behind the lines. Thank God, Puss still had his and, by offering him some of my spoils, I got him to dig my sleeping hole, too.

As I listened to old Puss cussing while he fought tree roots to dig our foxholes, I thought of the lorry ride through Meaux that day with the cheering crowds who enthusiastically greeted us wherever we went and the petite mademoiselle who'd asked me to return when the war was over.

As I sat waiting to bed down in the foxhole that Puss was digging, I searched in my pockets for the scrap of paper but it was gone, lost, no doubt, somewhere on the weary way we'd made today.

Puss stopped my daydreaming in no uncertain words. "Damn it all, Zebbie, you're always sittin' around dreamin' 'bout pretty women or scribblin' in your notebooks. Can't you gimme a hand with these damned roots?"

As I bent to help him, I got a whiff of something unusual.

"Puss, do you smell gas?"

"Yeah, sure do."

I was the NCO in charge of ordering gas masks!

"Gas!" I screamed at the top of my lungs. I put on my own mask and went scrambling to search for the shell that had delivered the gas. Part of my duty was to find any gas shell and hang it on a tree where it would be seen and serve as a warning to the troops. I couldn't find it, but I went up and down the line to see that the men had donned their masks. Satisfied that I had acquitted myself well in this first encounter with the insidious gas, I made my way back to my own dugout and settled down to await the all clear, which soon came.

Suddenly, a shot rang out very near to us.

"That was one of ours, Zeb," Puss said and we crawled out of our makeshift beds to investigate. We found one of the new—very young—recruits from Texas, staring in shock at his hand as blood spurted from the place where three of his fingers had been.

A sergeant from another outfit, whom we'd privately labeled "Sergeant Big-Mouth," also came running to investigate.

"What happened?" he growled.

The boy just looked at his ruined hand.

"What happened?" the sergeant demanded for the second time.

The kid finally said, "Ah don't know; ah was just cleaning my gun and it went off—"

"I think you figured shooting your fingers off was a good way to get out of fightin'," the sergeant said, disdainfully. "Well, you're right. You'll be discharged all right. But it will be dishonorably. And you'll do a hitch in jail, too."

The kid looked up, furious. "Ah ain't yellow, Sarge. Ah never had a gun in my hands before until a few days ago at Liverpool. Ah never went to do it; ah jest didn't realize it was loaded."

"Tell it to the marines, buddy."

But, just then the boy's own sergeant—an enormous Texan—came onto the scene. He took it all in, listened to the first sergeant's accusations, then shook his head.

"Ah know this boy, Sarge," he said, levelly, hitching up his pants. "If he says it was an accident, then, by God, it was an accident. Ah don't much appreciate you callin' one o' my boys yellow."

The bullying sergeant backed off a little. "Well, if you're willing to vouch for him, I guess we'll send him home with an honorable discharge," he said and went back to his own post.

I suppose you couldn't really blame the NCO for suspecting self-mutilation; as the fighting grew hotter and tension mounted, it *did* happen. But, like the big Texas sergeant, I just didn't believe it had in this case.

Like all good war stories, this one has a sequel, although, knowing the propensity of Texans to turn everything into a myth, I can't swear to its veracity. I ran into the big Texas sergeant after the battle of Jauglonne. He said that, during the heaviest bombardment, he'd come upon the big-mouthed sergeant, cowering and sobbing with fear in a dugout.

"Ah jest told him, 'Shoot a few fingers off, Sarge; it's a hell of a good way to get outta' fightin'.'"

In the morning, after our first night under fire, we could see French farmers stoically planting their fields, doing their level best to ignore the shells exploding so near and the possibility of German land mines on their own farms. I suppose there was nothing else they could do; the spectre of hunger during the coming winter, if they failed to plant now, was a powerful incentive to bravery. We saw that we were camped in an apple orchard where the fully leafed trees helped hide us from enemy reconnoitering planes.

Our own rations were woefully low since the provision wagons—which couldn't move as fast as men on foot could—were sixty miles behind us. Each man's daily ration consisted of a small square of salt pork and a few small potatoes which we tried to cook in our mess pans over twig fires.

The mule-powered kitchen wagon, driven by Red Gray, finally pulled into camp late one afternoon amid a pouring rain and the cheers of us all. Within a short time, the cooks were ladling thin soup into our mess kits. At least we had hot food, such as it was, before bedding down in the rain.

And, for once, the ever-busy artillery was silent.

CHAPTER 4

First Contact at the Front

After the worst night we'd yet endured in France—with rain pouring down, adding to the puddles in the bottom of our dugouts—we repacked our wet bedrolls. The eerie silence still holding, we marched toward Chateau-Thierry. By the time we'd stopped for our first rest, the sun had taken pity on a bunch of miserable doughboys and shone brightly. As we dried our blankets and packs in its warmth, a detachment of French infantrymen arrived with a consignment of Chauchat rifles, sixteen to a company.

For the rest of the day, we exhanged souvenirs and what small talk we could manage with the poilus. One youngster with a neat caterpillar mustache traded me a German jackknife with a black ebony handle for the fountain pen I'd bought from the jilted sergeant. They, who'd been at war for years, were loaded with belt buckles bearing the legend, "Gott Mit Uns" and officers' spiked helmets. After they left us, we settled into our bedrolls. The next day, July 4, was to be a day of rest in honor of our own national holiday. Instead, we were awakened at 2 AM and ordered to fall in quickly for a march to the front.

The 1st Brigade led off; we, the 2nd Brigade, followed immediately. When we reached the road, staff officers on horseback set the pace which— to soldiers burdened with 70-pound packs and their rifles—seemed sure to kill us before we ever encountered the enemy. The colonel and his staff kept moving along the line on horseback, urging us on.

"Step lively, boys, step lively!" they'd command. Easy for them to say! At each brief rest they ordered, staggering, gasping soldiers dropped where they stood.

We didn't reach the Grande Forest until daybreak the following day. By this time, there were many stragglers. As each man reached the shelter of the beautiful trees—France's only stretch of virgin forest—he dropped to the fragrant pine needles and fell instantly asleep. This forced march, by the entire 28th Division, had to be one of the most heroic epics of the war.

At three o'clock in the morning of July 5, we were ordered back to Bussieres. We'd no sooner gotten there, grumbling all the way, when we were ordered to return to our former posts.

"Officers must ha' made their brains tired ridin' on them all day," one weary private groused.

Our first encounter with the enemy after our gallant run was fairly brief. The 2nd Battalion—being a backup in the battle—received few casualties: 2 dead and 8 wounded. Privates Joseph Austra and Jesse Greer were among the ten reported missing in action. Austra, from Mahanoy City, was later accounted for. During one of our rest stops, Austra didn't scramble fast enough to avoid being run down by a truck. He'd been in the rear of the march and none of us saw it happening. So, when he didn't answer roll call later, he was reported missing in action. Weeks later, we learned both his legs had been broken and he'd been taken to the hospital. Later, he rejoined the regiment. Private Jesse Greer was wounded but died later at the hospital. Private Strauss of Franklin and Private First Class Don White of Meadville were wounded.

Under heavy shellfire—which did considerable damage to the magnificent old trees—we remained for three days. The field kitchen caught up with us here and fed us magnificently. We were urged to eat all we could, since heaven alone knew when we'd get another chance.

At nightfall, July 9, we were ordered to leave the comparative shelter of the forest. Our destination was either Queue or Trinity Farms, just back of the front, where the ubiquitous trenches had dramatically changed the peaceful landscape. The Germans had been stopped in Belleau Wood by the 5th Marines and the regular army troops, reinforced by the 109th, 110th, and 111th National Guard Regiments of the 28th Pennsylvania Division.

Company F arrived at Queue Farm at about 6 PM on July 13, the eve of Bastille Day. The American High Command guessed that the Germans would expect the French to be celebrating their great national holiday—La Fete Nationale—and would likely press the attack to take advantage of it. A battery of Chauchats, the long-barreled 75 millimeter French guns, awaited the attack on the flagstone-paved courtyard. Behind us, the frame farmhouse showed the terrible effects of years of war, just as the fertile fields and woodlands of the farm did. We spent the remaining hours of daylight and most of the next day preparing for the Germans' threatened "Fiedensturm," or peace drive which was to capture Paris and sever the Allied armies, breaking the back of the resistance forever.

By 4 PM on the following day, the blue-clad French poilus had fused and stacked great piles of the long, slender brass shells around their big guns. Though we knew a great offensive would begin that night, for the time being there was a spell of comparative quiet. Some of us ambled over to chat with the poilus, who greeted us with broad smiles. One of them, in a mixture of French and English, said, "Beaucoup souvenirs for Allemands tonight," and offered me a drink of vin rouge from the bottle he had on hand. As the Allied High Command surmised, the French soldiers were celebrating Bastille Day, but I couldn't see that it impaired their ability to load and fire their weapons. Throughout the ensuing battle, these big French guns—eight of them—situated directly behind our trenches, kept up a continual bombardment until their barrels nearly melted.

Throughout the night, we non-coms stationed our men in the trenches—with gas masks at hand—and then went up and down them to familiarize ourselves with the trench system. I noticed that the dugout assigned to Lieutenant Thompson remained empty. During the entire engagement that was to come, I never saw him take advantage of its greater safety; he stayed in the trenches with his men.

When some of the NCOs, including Sergeant Louis "Brownie" Knode and myself, had done all we could to settle our men to await the expected assault, we returned to the old house to investigate French eating and, especially, drinking customs. The French soldiers had finished stockpiling shells and were having an early supper on the porch. With cordial smiles and gestures, they invited us to join them. Brownie remarked that there were definite advantages to being an NCO in wartime.

After sampling their food and wine, we found ourselves hardly able to keep our eyes open. The poilus urged us to rest awhile on several crude bunks they'd fashioned throughout the farmhouse and adjoining buildings. Fatigued from our long march of the day and, perhaps, feeling the effect of the vin, I stretched out on a cot in the kitchen and soon dozed off.

At about 4 PM, I awakened with a jerk when the bombardment suddenly increased in volume. Blinking sleep from my eyes, I saw Private First Class Oren "Red" Berlin lying across the door sill. I got up to go to his assistance when an enormous explosion, right in the courtyard, shook the old house. I felt a blow like a sledge hammer between my shoulder blades and felt hot blood running down my back. Dazed, I staggered back to the bunk.

Sergeant Knode, who'd been trying to escape the noise by sleeping in an outbuilding farther from the guns, came running in. Seeing me sprawled on the bunk, he yelled, "Where are you hit?"

"Never mind me; look at Berlin, there."

He ran to comply. "Too late for the poor devil," he shouted. He came back to me. "Let's see the damage," he said and pulled up my shirt and jacket. "Not too bad, Zeb. Just a bit o' shrapnel." He rummaged in his pack and found the iodine and bandages which we all carried and soon had an emergency bandage on me. "Now, let's get over to the trenches."

He helped me to my feet and, stepping over poor Oren's body, we left the farmhouse. In the courtyard, the French soldiers were struggling to hitch the few horses not already killed by the barrage to the two guns still undamaged. We made our way past them, stumbling over an American soldier lying in a ditch. We tried to help him but it was too late for him. At last, we reached the woods and dropped into the nearest trench and secured our gas masks.

High explosives and gas shells were falling thick as hail. I watched, peering over the edge of the trench, as a big artillery horse, stumbling over its own intestines hanging from a washtub-sized hole in its belly, tried to escape the hellish shelling. Another horse, a beautiful bay, also wounded, jumped in circles. Sergeant Cutshall, who was within shooting range of them, ended their suffering with two well-placed bullets. I blessed God for the man's proficiency on the pistol range.

The nausea and dizziness my wound had caused being manageable, I started my rounds to check on the boys of my own squad. To my dismay, I found that Private Frank Homman—a lad who'd worked as a printing apprentice under me at the *Daily New Era*—had been killed as well as an Indiana private named Emanuel Swanson, a recent battalion replacement, and Private Clarence Ritter of Macungie. Frank was the first Company F mortality from Huntingdon. Later, the Huntingdon American Legion Post was named for him. He had been the only survivor of the scouting party that had killed Jesse Greer and wounded Privates Strauss and White.

Sergeant Cutshall and I went to the aid of Private Elmer Murdock of Franklin, Pennsylvania, when a shell blew him right out of the trench. We could do nothing for him except to stay with him until his badly-mangled body stopped twitching. This was my first experience of watching one of my buddies "go west," which was the doughboys' euphemism for dying, the ultimate trip home.

The continuous bombardment was nigh unendurable. During this "Peace Drive," I think, virtually every man suffered to some degree from what we called shell shock . . . what our sons in a later war would call battle fatigue. I know I did. For years after the war, I would awaken suddenly and leap from bed—scaring the wits out of my poor wife—certain I was back in France, under heavy fire.

This, our first encounter with trench warfare, was generally acknowledged to be one of the most fearsome engagements of the AEF's stay in France. Normally, we'd have been "broken in" at a less intense pace. As it was, we went "over the top" several times that night.

Back in the trenches, I sought out Lieutenant Thompson to report our casualties.

He nodded sadly. "I hate to impose on you, Corporal, but would you mind taking a report of our losses back to battalion headquarters?"

The polite request, effective as any direct command to those of us who loved Lieutenant Thompson, was always his way.

I had not progressed fifty feet through the hell of falling shells when another terrifying barrage began to pummel us. I was alone in the woods and I don't mind admitting, scared half to death. I spent more time on my belly, trying to protect myself from more flying shrapnel, than walking erect. I think I would have quit and run back to the comparative safety of the trenches but I just couldn't imagine facing the Lieutenant whom I so much admired without having completed the task he'd sent me on. The entire journey probably took no more than fifteen minutes but I felt as if I'd been in that dark wood, with hellishly screaming shells falling all around me, for many hours. At last, I reached battalion headquarters where four men were guarding the entrance to the dugout with fixed bayonets. Sergeant Patrick Shields, swearing in a continuous streak, stood near the entrance to the dugout, shooting off flares one after another.

"Where's the Major?" I yelled.

He stopped his flare shooting long enough to gesture toward the dugout entrance. I pushed aside the blanket door and crawled down a steep incline, bumping my head against a wooden door at the end. I banged with the handle of my 45 against the wooden door to be heard above the bombardment.

"Come in," said a voice. I entered and saw the commander of the 2nd Battalion, sitting alone beside a wooden crate on which burned a single candle.

I made my report but he didn't seem to be paying much attention. I stood at attention, awaiting his dismissal. Finally, he said, "Tell Thompson that we're trying to get word back to the artillery details that they're shooting short of the target. When you have given him the message, bring me back a report on current conditions at Thompson's post."

With sinking heart, I saluted and went out. I'd made it through that hell once and had to return. The very thought of a second mission through what proved to be the heaviest bombardment American troops would have to undergo during the entire war turned my blood to ice.

This time, I decided to make a mad run for it, flopping to the ground only when an especially shrill whistling heralded the proximity of a shell about to explode close to me. Somehow, I did make it back in one piece. When I gave Lieutenant Thompson the Major's message and added that he'd told me to return to him, the Lieutenant looked up at the exploding shells and snorted.

"Forget it, Corporal," he said flatly. "If he wants another report on conditions here, he can come for it himself."

I couldn't stop the grin from spreading across my face. Sure, I'd dreamed of gallantry in the field and the resultant glory. But only a fool would send men through that barrage for such a flimsy reason. I thanked God that Lieutenant Thompson had his men's welfare more at heart than the Major did. With a sharp salute, I left Lieutenant Thompson and returned to my own squad to wait for the end of the barrage and the probable attack of the Hun infantry.

The Fifth German Offensive lasted for twelve straight hours. They poured everything they had into it, knowing it to be their last chance to take Paris before America's full strength arrived. Indeed, 41 of their divisions—a total of more than 550,000 men, two to our one—actually crossed the Marne River at a few places, but were stopped cold by the Allied armies—many of them unseasoned AEF doughboys—and forced back to the other side.

Wounded in this terrible engagement included Private First Class Isaac Steel, one of the boys who'd been with Company F on the border and transferred to the 110th Regiment at Camp Hancock, Corporals Edward Gribben, Carl Hays, and Fred Smith of Franklin, Private Donald Johnston and Corporal Dorris Figard of Huntingdon, Privates Elmer "Impy Dog" Feaster and George Gibboney of Huntingdon, Harry Estep of Shy Beaver, south of Huntingdon, John Brown of Oklahoma and William Hamel of Alexandria, west of Huntingdon, Philip Short, a Huntingdon boy with another company, and Private First Class Roy Crownover. The following day, Private Harold Helsel suffered from gas burns and inhalation, spending a short time in the hospital tent. Later, while trying to scale a high cliff, Helsel received a neck wound and, in the Argonne Forest, took a second bullet in the chest, which caused him to be invalided home. Also injured by gas was Private Lorenzo Stevens, one of our replacements from Kentucky.

When the battle had subsided enough, the cooks quickly supplied a hot meal. Empty as our stomachs were, few among us could eat much; we weren't inured to the horrible sights and smells of battle all around us.

The sun being hot, Corporal Bob White organized the grave-digging detail. Nearly all able-bodied men helped gather their fallen comrades, taking them to a point near the dressing station for temporary burial. No men were ever handled with more love and respect. The dead horses and mules were another matter. Men, already nearing the point of exhaustion, dug enormous pits and dragged the pathetic carcasses into them. The beasts' long legs posed a problem. In the dire necessity of interring the rapidly decaying corpses, we had no alternative but to chop off the stiff legs and lay them beside the stark bodies. By dark, we had all the bodies buried. But, even with a stiff breeze blowing over the battlefield, by morning, the smell was nearly overpowering. This omnipresent smell was one of the most horrifying things about war.

As we fell in to pursue the enemy, the panorama of war, worse than our wildest imaginings, nearly unmanned us. We saw ambulances overturned, their cargo of wounded men—some still on their stretchers—now beyond all help. Tanks, twisted and useless, sat silent with their crews hanging dead from the tops of them; field artillery, battered into useless junk, their firing crews bloating corpses in the hot sun, the stench . . . the overwhelming stench that made us fight to keep our gorges down, and, most horrifying of all, the clouds of vultures circling lazily in the azure sky over the battlefield . . . props in a morality play about the futility of war.

Several miles from Queue Farm, we caught up with the retreating Germans. A half dozen French 75s—with mud-caked Americans taking their turns operating them—were lined up in an open field. Another crew of gunners lay in the mud, sleeping as soundly as if in their own beds back home instead of almost under the thundering guns. Having lived through my first big battle, my preconceptions about the lot of artillerymen were changing drastically. Like most infantry soldiers in the midst of a grousing session, I'd often given it as my opinion that the artillery boys had it made. While we foot soldiers were slogging through the mud, they rode horseback. Even if they did have to walk, they could entrust *their* seventy-pound packs to the horses or gunnery wagons.

But they couldn't dive into the nearest trench under fire either; they had to stand by their guns, often literally keeling over from weariness before replacements came to relieve them.

The closer we came to the front, the more nightmarish became the landscape. We saw heaps of bodies where a German shell had wiped out an entire platoon, a shoe with its owner's foot still inside, dead horses and mules, shattered cottages and trees. And hundreds of blankets, bedrolls, cameras, binoculars whose owners would never reclaim them. We had been warned not to pick up such items; the Germans frequently booby-trapped them, but some men did so anyhow. There were heaps of abandoned German artillery shells everywhere: slender 77s, five-foot long railway car shells, hand grenades with handles which the doughboys called potato mashers. They looked like small salmon tins with nine-inch hollowed-out wooden handles through which a detonating wire was strung. Hooks on the edge of each grenade made it easy to carry on a soldier's belt.

I looked around in horrified disbelief. Doomsday itself could be no worse than this hell. How had we Huntingdon County boys ever thought war was glamorous?

By evening, we'd reached a forest northeast of Charly on the Marne River where division headquarters was established. A good stiff breeze was blowing the ever-present odor of death away at last. We deployed through the trees and looked down upon the nearly-destroyed town of Chateau-Thierry. Before the first battle of the Marne, it had been a community of about 7,000 souls, roughly the same size as Huntingdon. Now, scarcely one house remained intact. And it was still under bombardment from our own troops because the German rear guard had holed up there, stubbornly defying the Allied advance.

We made camp on this height, overlooking the town. All night long, we watched star shells, falling gently to earth on little silk parachutes. No fourth of July extravaganza we had ever imagined could touch this display of explosives. Finally, tormented by lice, hungry, exhausted, many of us slipped quietly over the bank in the dark and clambered down to the water. We stripped off our filthy clothes and plunged into the muddy water. Despite the roiled-up condition of it, it felt cool and welcome.

However, our movements dislodged the bodies of dead enemy soldiers and they floated up around us like so many lifeless, swollen porpoises. Despite our misery, we scrambled out of the water and in among the trees, where we settled down for the night.

Soon enough, we were ordered to pack up and wait for nightfall. As soon as it was dark enough to cover our movements, we left the forest and marched to the highway where a line of empty transport trucks awaited us. We piled into them and rolled through the darkness for two hours, alighting at a small village called Chezy.

"We'll bivouac here until daylight, men," Lieutenant Thompson murmured. "No talking or smoking. In fact, make as little noise as possible. We're very close to the front."

We camped gladly. Though we weren't as physically exhausted as we'd been after our first major skirmish, the uncertainty of when we'd next see combat was telling on us.

No bugles sounded reveille in the morning, but, in truth, none was needed. Satan himself couldn't have chosen a more uncomfortable bivouac than the stony undergrowth-choked land beneath us. But the wonderful breakfast the cooks had prepared made up for it. There was hot oatmeal sweetened with real molasses, fried bacon, and hot coffee. Each man was also issued a box of real chocolate candy. No one knew whence the latter treat had come but, believe me, there was many a fervent prayer of thanksgiving mentioning the unknown benefactor. Nothing tasted better to a fighting man than chocolate candy.

We were ordered to stay there all day, resting until dark. Then we were issued extra rations and spare bandoliers of ammunition. We were heading into battle again.

CHAPTER 5

Death Valley

With only starlight—and an occasional exploding shell—to guide us, we marched across land that had sometime previously been a battleground.

Poets write of twinkling stars against the vast curtain of the night, evoking fantasies of peace and love. As I looked up at the star-filled sky above, I was caught in just such a reverie. I couldn't help but think of how often each Company F boy had used to sit with a special young lady on her front porch at home—if very lucky—holding her hand. Perhaps he would point out the Big Dipper, the North Star, and, growing a bit bolder, Venus, the star of love. Memories of those long-gone nights under other star-filled skies, while—here and now—the very earth shook from the reverberations of cannon, were enough to make a man weep in the dark.

I looked up and wondered if those I loved back home were gazing at the same stars and thinking of me: my parents and siblings, girls I'd courted, even my old black and tan hound, Sailor.

No, of course they weren't gazing at the stars; back home, it was yesterday. With a sigh, I hoisted my pack more securely and headed into the woods where the stars were hidden from view. As I marched with my comrades in arms, I dreamed of happier days, back home, where there were no bloody battles, no screams of dying friends and horses. I shut my eyes for a moment and wished I might fall asleep and awaken to find this "war to end all wars" was just a bad dream. Later, back home, I found the following poem I'd written, on a dirty scrap of envelope, after that night march.

NIGHT SKY OVER A BATTLEFIELD

In muddy khaki, crouching, dodging, ducking low,
   Cowering in a shell hole
While explosions vicious and violent
   Roll, like rumbling thunder.

The terrifying screech of giant shells
    Set nerves a-quiver, flesh a-creeping
And you're sure war is truly hell, but by
    The grace of God . . . with you, all's well.
Star-shells soar high and twinkle,
    Brilliantly lighting a jet-black sky
Revealing war's horrors in the making,
    Hate, the fury of vengeance. Oh, God, why
Must so many brave young soldiers die?

But morning came at last. Daylight found us still marching and revealed a long, long line of doughboys ahead and behind me, strung out along what had once been a smooth, wide highway that the French had been justifiably proud of. Now, the road was pitted by shell holes, littered with the debris of war. Stone bridges that had once spanned quiet streams lay in ruins all along our way, sometimes necessitating detours. Farmhouses that had stood for generations lined the way, stark and ruined with gaping holes in roofs and walls, sometimes, nothing more than heaps of rubble.

We hiked all day on this road, mostly drenched from the rain . . . France's everlasting rain . . . which had returned. During one rest period, I checked my map and realized we were on the main road back to Chateau-Thierry. When I mentioned the fact to Bob Appleby, he said, "Can anyone tell me why we march endless miles all day and night to get back to a town we left yesterday?"

Nobody could, of course.

Late in the afternoon of July 24, we reached the town, spread out on two sides of the Marne. To our horror, we soon found that the makeshift bridge that spanned the river was the target of the Germans' long-range guns. Since there was no other way into town, we crossed it, losing several of the men from the battalion to a bursting shell. One Company E man accidently kicked one of their deadly potato mashers which exploded, wounding him and several of his squad. Privates Bill English and Fred Drolsbaugh of Huntingdon were also injured.

As we neared the town, I smelled gas and sounded the alarm; we donned the hated gas masks. MPs (Military Police) stationed at each intersection directed us through the town on the northward road. When we'd gone six kilometers, the officers called a halt for the night and we dropped like stones to the hard ground. At dawn, we were on our way again, passing through increasingly desolate landscapes.

Our platoon sergeant, Kaspher Moyer, led us off to the left through a trampled wheat field, into a section of Belleau Wood where a party of trench-digging infantrymen had stopped for breakfast. Some of our boys, not to miss a meal, thrust their mess kits out in front of the cooks who good-naturedly filled them until the resulting bottleneck in our line made Sergeant Moyer call a halt to the mooching.

After another mile, we were ordered to fall out and lay aside our full packs, taking only our combat packs which consisted only of mess kits, extra ammo and our razors. With pounding hearts, we fixed bayonets and began moving forward. Orders were to await the next barrage, then bound forward under its cover. But it failed to materialize. Finally, our sergeants ordered us to advance in skirmish formation.

We moved slowly forward for nearly seven kilometers without encountering any enemy except for a wounded soldier we found in a dugout. He could—or would—tell us nothing of the Germans' position; we assumed they were retreating rapidly ahead of our advance.

However, we'd lost contact with the French who were supposed to be on our left, so a halt was called until we could reestablish contact with them. Our officers realized the peril of getting too far separated from our allies.

As we waited, units from the 111th came up behind us. They were supposed to be ahead of us so it was apparent that the march had become badly disorganized. Like soldiers everywhere, we groused loudly about the lack of leadership among . . . not *our* officers, you understand, but "theirs." The truth was, the 112th had lost a number of officers: Captain James Henderson of Oil City, commander of Company D was killed; 1st Battalion commander, Major Charles B. Smathers was gassed; Captain Lucius Phelps, wounded; Second Lieutenant Harold Speakman, killed; Lieutenant Colonel Robert B. Gamble, Major Charles Hogan, and Captain Rasselas W. Brown were all evacuated, leaving no field officers except our doughty Colonel George C. Rickards who quickly named other officers to take the place of those he'd lost. At last a semblance of order was established and the two regiments moved swiftly over the gloomy, swampy land.

By dark, scattered machine-gun fire had slowed us almost to a standstill. We were ordered to fall out and dig trenches for the night. The entire 112th was now in a sort of valley and, from the heavy shelling, we surmised the Germans had found our range. There was no escaping it however and we were subjected to heavy shelling throughout that long night. Company E lost several soldiers and one lieutenant. A Company F private, Carlton Cowher, from Mapleton Depot, a village a few miles southeast of Huntingdon, crawled out in a futile attempt to help one of his buddies from Company E. He was hit by a piece of shrapnel. Private George Godard and another stretcher-bearer braved the bombardment to carry him back. But Cowher died before they reached the first-aid station.

When daylight came, some officers from the 32nd Division made their way to our position and demanded to know who our commanding officer was.

"Captain Phelps, 112th Regiment, 28th Division, Sir," Sergeant Moyer said, saluting.

A big major, ranking officer of the group made a gesture of exasperation and began to swear.

"Find him at once. Tell him to get his people the hell out of this sector," he snapped.

"I can't do that, Sir. Captain Phelps was wounded last night and has been taken to the rear."

"Well, then, who's in command here?"

Sergeant Moyer said, "I suppose I am, Sir."

"Well, you're in no-man's-land of the 32nd Division sector. Order your men to get the hell out of here."

That was all the command we needed. Every man within range of the major's booming voice promptly got "the hell out of there." Till then, we'd hardly supposed it mattered *where* you fought the Boche.

Most of Company F managed to find their own kitchen wagons where we were given a breakfast of stale bread and cheese. We reunited with Lieutenant Thompson and informed him of our close call, at which he expressed deep relief that we'd had only the one casualty.

Within an hour, Captain Harry Miller, in command after Phelps was wounded, led the advance to our own sector from which we could clearly see the retreating Germans. On the way, we passed whole lines of German prisoners, who waved and smiled, apparently quite happy to be out of the fray, even though it meant they were prisoners.

Lieutenants Thompson and Earl Sanders ordered us to rest while, with Jimmy Bottomfield, they reconnoitered. We gratefully obeyed. When they returned, we followed them to the left of the swampy section where we'd spent the previous night and onto a fairly intact highway with deep ditches along each side. But, shortly, a German observation balloon spotted us and reported our position. Immediately, we were bombarded with 77 millimeter shells which sent us diving for the shelter of the ditches. Thank goodness, their aim was poor. Then, a French flyer shot down the balloon, allowing us to continue along the road in comparative safety.

Almost immediately, an orderly on horseback brought us a command from headquarters that we were to about-face and return to the area where we'd left our blanket rolls and heavier packs the day before.

"The God-damned brass who're running this war haven't got enough gray matter between their ears to lead a pack o' hogs to an acorn tree," groused one doughboy.

"Who the hell ever heard of an acorn tree?" jibed another.

Private First Class Bob Appleby, our fatherly philosopher, stopped the discussion. With a broad smile, he said, "Listen, you featherbrains, we'll muddle through. God always looks after fools like us and idiots like officers."

We found our bedrolls but not our kitchen wagons, so rolled up, supperless, to sleep that night. By the time the kitchens caught up to us in the morning, we were ravenous.

When nighttime fell, we were ordered to march out "artillery fashion," that is, single file, ten paces between men. This time, our direction was northward on the highway, our destination . . . anyone's guess. Private First Class Bob Appleby suspected it would be Fismes, a German stronghold on the Vesle River, which was the last barrier to Germany itself. So far, the Huns had churned up all the rest of Europe, but their own homeland hadn't endured mangling.

As usual, rain fell on us in torrents as we trudged through the black night. During a rest stop, Corporal Roy Sellers, one of the replacements from Oklahoma, like Private Austra earlier, was hit by a truck driving without lights. An ambulance coming from the front with a load of wounded, stopped to pick him up.

The pace was grueling. Our officers urged us on continually, telling us we had to be across a stretch of open land ahead and safely into the forest before daybreak, when the observation balloons could spot us. The men were falling from exhaustion and, as dawn came, many stragglers had not yet reached cover. But, for once, the rain and fog had proved a blessing, hiding us from the German observation balloons. Miraculously, we'd moved an army and their equipment without being spotted by the enemy.

When our officers finally called a halt, many of the men began building small fires, anxious to dry out bedding and clothing, but orders to douse them raced through our ranks immediately. So we ate a soggy breakfast, grumbling between bites. Almost immediately, a French regiment joined us and we started toward Fismes.

At Dravagny, the regimental brass set up headquarters but the lettered companies continued on for several kilometers. When we were ordered to halt, we began digging shelters along the eastern bank of the road as our trucks pulled off to the other side to wait for our planes to spot the German artillery that was shelling the road ahead of us and, we hoped, take it out. Coming toward us from Fismes was a long line of the walking wounded. Frequently, they would stumble to the side of the road so that lorry-loads of even more seriously wounded doughboys could be taken to the first-aid station in the rear. And, all the while, they—and we—dodged vicious little Minnenwerfer missiles.

As the men of the 112th Division watched these boys making their torturous way to the rear, we silently questioned the officers who'd kept us running all over Hell's half-acre—always around the perimeter of battle—the past few days while the 32nd Division, obviously, needed help. As if in answer to our unspoken criticism, they ordered us to get some sleep; soon we'd be relieving the 32nd.

So, amidst the falling shells and the moans of the wounded, we rolled up in our blankets and slept.

Lieutenant Thompson's "Fall in, boys," brought us to instant wakefulness. Nothing had changed; the rain was still falling on the weary, mudspattered soldiers coming from the front. We fell in and followed Lieutenant Thompson as he left the road and struck out through swampy ground. Judging from the steadily increasing sound of artillery, we realized we were coming closer and closer to the source of the bombardment. Suddenly, an explosion even louder than usual boomed.

"Easy, boys, it's a big one, from down in the valley," came a shout from near the head of the column. "Take cover—you'll find it. We'll wait for dawn."

We deployed ourselves into hundreds of small foxholes, evidently recently vacated, on the hillside of the valley. Below us, the Allies' artillery kept hammering away at the German position along the Vesle River. We soon discovered that, by watching closely, we could see the red fire as shells left the massive muzzles of the big guns.

When, at last, the sun came up, we discovered our hillside position was unshaded and totally exposed. Millions of huge flies swarmed over us—and the blood we saw all around—making our lives miserable. There were French engineers everywhere with many pontoons, waiting on wagons to be hauled forward and used to construct bridges across the Vesle River. To our chagrin, no order to advance was forthcoming. Indeed, as several days passed, leaving us stranded on the hillside, exposed to mustard-gas attack, we learned first hand what the army's favorite command— "hurry up and wait"—really meant. Before the engagement was over, the valley, Fond de Mezieres, came to be called "Death Valley" because of the many casualties we suffered there.

One of the artillerymen below us climbed up to our position during his rest period. His stories of the big guns' proficiency sounded like tall tales at first; after a few days, with the bird's-eye view we had of the awful destruction they could wreak, we believed everything he said.

Private Jimmy White, he who we'd gotten so drunk on the road to Paris, didn't hold a grudge; mess kit tucked into the front of his blouse, he found me during this hellishly tedious wait on the hillside. As we sat side by side in my foxhole, watching the grim panorama in front of us, a German shell screamed down close beside us, hitting a shelter tent where two men had been sleeping. To our horror, we saw one man blown high in the air, his body going asunder as he fell. Yet, almost miraculously, his tent mate crawled from the remnants of the tent, and headed for the shelter of the woods behind us. Before Jimmy and I could follow, another shell struck right beside an officer on horseback. The rider, with both legs below the knee blown away, sailed into the air but the horse galloped off, apparently unharmed.

The stretcher-bearers were there at once and ran into the woods with the injured man.

Getting out of this section of the hillside seemed the better part of valor at the moment so Jimmy and I decided to visit Corporal Bill "Sand Googie" Holder, who'd dubbed me Zebediah on the border. At Camp Hancock, Bill had been assigned to the 107th Machine-gun Battalion, which was now deployed near the top of a neighboring hill. Jimmy and I found Bill beside his 60 calibre gun, enjoying a lull in the action at that point. He was overjoyed to see us, declaring we were the first Company F boys he'd seen since leaving Hancock. We sat and talked for some time, wondering if we'd ever go over the top. Bill told us of a loss, tragic to one of our mule skinners, Red Gray. One of Red's beloved, mouse-gray mules had been killed as Red tried to bring us a cooked meal while we lay on the hillside.

"Was Red hurt?" I asked, anxiously.

"Naw. But the mule fell on him and he had so much blood on him when they got him free of the beast, we couldn't be sure for awhile. 'Sides, he kept swearing so bad, we couldn't get any sense outa' him for a time."

"Because he'd lost his faithful old mule?" Jimmy asked.

Bill shook his head. "Well, that, o' course. Damned near cried when he saw his ol' 'Mountain Canary' was done for. But mostly 'cause he swallowed his chaw!"

Despite the chaos around us, thinking of ol' Red choking on his baseball-sized quid of tobacco made us smile a little.

At last, Jimmy, who played the flute in the regimental band, declared he had a long way to go before dark and left us as we sent our best to another Company F man, Bill Edwards, who had also been assigned to the regimental band after recovering from a serious injury in a training accident at Camp Hancock, though his brother, Bob, was still with Company F.

I noticed Sand Googie wiping a tear from his eye. In a little while, I, too, said my farewells and headed back to my own hole on the hillside. I hated to leave a Huntingdon boy all alone at his gun, but, as the poilus said, "C'est le guerre."

The Germans knew that America's entry into the war had turned the tide at last and they fought with all the fury of desperate men. It was several days before the German supply base at Fere-en-Tardenois finally fell to parts of the Rainbow and the 32nd Division. Thereafter, the German retreat was rapid.

On Sunday, August 4, after a good, cooked breakfast and being given candy and cigarettes by the Red Cross, we picked up our packs and set off in rapid pursuit. At last, we were to relieve the 32nd Division, get a chance to pay Fritz back for our dead buddies, and the gassed and wounded ones, too.

Headquarters Company and Regimental P.C. had stalled along the Jauglonne-Fere-en-Tardenois Road, due to rain and darkness. Near here, at a little town called Chamery, flying-ace Lieutenant Quentin Roosevelt, son of our late president, had been shot down. His grave had already become a sort of shrine to American doughboys. But, at last, our Divison was chasing the enemy from Fresnes, Courmont, Cierges, Chamery, Coulonges, Cohan, and Dravagny.

Our forces couldn't understand the uncanny way the Germans always aimed right at our units until an intelligence agent uncovered an old woman who'd been signaling them our position from the belfry of Dravagny's church, the only building still intact. Though, not as glamorous as Mata Hari, once she'd been apprehended, they lost their "eyes" and were unable to do such fearsome damage thereafter.

As we headed toward the front, we were delighted to hear that the 108th American Artillery would be our support unit during our advance to the Vesle River. Up until now, we'd had to rely on the French artillery units, and, though they were reliable and tough, we just wanted our own countrymen to cover us. Besides, the language barrier often made communication difficult.

By evening, we were within sight of the Vesle. However, our march was halted by a heavy German barrage on the road ahead of us which had pounded the French engineers and their pontoons mercilessly. The 32nd Division had fought their way to Fismes on the river and, despite tremendous casualties, were doggedly holding the southern two-thirds of the city. However, their strength was flagging and the battle was now at a standoff. We had now been in France nearly three months. Already, America had made a great difference in the way the war was going and we were determined to make even more. Now, we would soon relieve the 32nd; it was up to us Pennsylvanians to turn the tide in the Allies' favor.

The Minnenwerfers were active but, luckily for us, a little off target. They did manage to hit the ammunition limber Red Gray, with a new "Mountain Canary" in the shafts, was driving. There was no doubt about it, Red led a charmed life. Once again, though a mechanic named George Agnew, from Franklin, Pennsylvania, was riding atop the ammo and had his leg nearly severed by flying shrapnel, Red came through without a scratch. I don't know whether he swallowed his chaw that time, though.

Fortunately, despite the shelling and resultant delays, we had no further casualties. We had, frequently, to allow south-bound ambulances to pass us as we made our halting way to a town called St. Giles, formerly a large German supply and ammunition depot as well as a large base hospital for the enemy soldiers.

Three battalions of the 112th entered the line from different angles. Our own, the 2nd Battalion, kept to the main road into Fismes where the weary 32nd Division happily greeted us, their relief. The exhausted men lost little time getting back to Death Valley, now safe from shelling, to rest. The other two battalions veered off to the right away from us.

The men from Companies E, F, and G swarmed into Fismes at about three in the afternoon. We had orders to search every tiny nook and corner, to rout out any lingering Germans.

Senses alert, fearful of ambush, I dodged from doorway to doorway, and was suddenly astonished by the sound of piano music coming from a big, brick house whose roof was half blown away. Mesmerized, I followed the sound into the wide central hallway of the house and looked through a double door into a large, littered parlor. There, seated at a magnificent piano, was a mud-spattered doughboy, playing confidently . . . some lovely classical piece that I couldn't identify. Beside him, as entranced as I, stood another soldier, listening intently. There was something nearly sacred about sounds so beautiful rising to the heavens in the midst of this terrible devastation.

When the young pianist had finished the selection, I couldn't help applauding. The bewhiskered doughboy bowed his thanks as if he'd been in the Metropolitan Opera House, even as he flashed me a bright smile and again laid his hands upon the keys. This time, he played an old familiar hymn, "In the Garden."

I felt tears trickling down my cheeks as I silently said the words I'd loved to hear my mother sing, along with the music: ". . . and He walks with me, and He talks with me, and He tells me I am His own . . ." Never, never, before or since, have the words had such meaning to me. Never had I felt such dependence on my Maker.

When the song was finished, I turned back to the task at hand and ran farther down toward the public square, where Puss Hawn, Ernest Meese and some other doughboys, who I didn't know, were examining something in the street. I approached to take a look. A huge, round marble pillar, one of four which supported the porch of the magnificent city hall, lay across the street. Protruding from beneath it, lay the khaki-clad arm of a doughboy, still clutching his rifle. A little farther, a dead German soldier sprawled on his back, an American bayonet, rifle still attached, protruding from his breast. Beside him lay the owner of the rifle, who'd evidently been shot or killed by flying shrapnel before he could draw out the bayonet.

But we had the Germans on the run. The battle line was drawn straight from Soissons to Reims; the danger to Paris was ended. And, for the first time since we'd landed in France, our division had been entrusted with a vital sector. We meant to conduct ourselves valiantly. Already, we had driven the enemy from Fismes on the south side of the river; they had retreated to Fismette on the north bank.

The Vesle River was only a few yards wide, really not much more than a "crick" by Pennsylvania standards. The bridge approaching it was a shambles, practically impassable to cars and trucks, yet it was the only way in or out of the town since the riverbed, too, proved to be unfordable, even where it was shallow enough, being filled with tangles of barbed wire.

The Vesle was the last barrier between us and a strongly fortified line of resistance through the town of Fismette on the other side of the river. A high hill rose behind the little town which was enclosed by a stone wall. Between the wall and the hill lay five hundred yards of trenches. For now, there was nothing much to do but wait for the engineers with their pontoon bridges to catch up so we could cross the river. We were champing at the bit to continue our pursuit of the Germans.

For the time being, the enemy was well aware of our positions and continually straffed the streets we'd already taken. On August 8, one of the Company F replacements, Private Christopher Gerve of New Hampshire, had been cut nearly in two by German shrapnel. The poor lad lived only a moment, begging us for water which we gladly gave him, only to have it run out the gaping hole in his middle, mixed with his life's blood. It was blessed relief when the boy died.

Private Harry Lukehart suffered a hit in the thigh which caused him to limp until his dying day. These casualties, however, were miraculously small, considering the ferocity of the attack. The town had been home to 7,000. When we arrived, about three-fourths of it had already been destroyed. When that night's attack was over, it was completely gone.

What a price we were paying for regaining a few square miles of French soil. But, for the first time since landing at Calais, the 28th, the Division the Germans had dubbed "the bucket of blood division," was holding a vital sector, awaiting only the order to advance against the foe.

And, as dark fell, the order came. Lieutenant Thompson shouted, "Rifle Grenade Squad, forward to the river. Fire your missiles, then start across. The rest of the company will follow."

"That's us, boys," I yelled, "attach bayonets and follow me."

CHAPTER 6

Crossing the Vesle River

With nerves keyed to the breaking point, we moved toward the bridge the engineers had thrown across the river. Sergeant Moyer was waiting near the hastily constructed span. We knew the Germans always left machine gunners and riflemen to cover a general retreat and we fully expected this situation would be no exception. Once the main army was safely away, the Boche rear guard in Fismette would certainly make a last stand.

"Put a grenade to the left of the bridge and a bit ahead of that point, then go ahead over," Moyer ordered calmly. "The rest of the company will be right behind you."

With the 109th Machine-gun Brigade providing our covering fire, we started across the makeshift bridge. The Germans were not done yet. Rifles kept up a constant fire ahead of us. Every second, we expected to be hit by the hidden riflemen and machine gunners waiting on the other side. When we were about halfway across, I heard cries for help and paused as I recognized two downed men, Private William Palmer of Franklin and a medical corpsman named Jeffries who'd been attached to Company F.

"Keep going, keep going; the medics will get them," someone behind me snapped.

Feeling great guilt at not seeing to them, I quickened my pace. Leaving wounded men was the hardest part of the war for me. Their cries seemed to ring in my ears long after I'd moved out of range. Later, I learned that Palmer had been shot through the kidneys. Indeed, there were many casualties that night as we crossed the river.

As we poured across the bridge from Fismes into Fismette, the machine-gun fire from the trenches and the Chateau de Diable beyond increased ominously, so fierce, in fact, that none of our companies were able to get across the bridge in any force, so those of us who had made it were on our own at first. Cut off as we were, we crouched in wrecked doorways or behind shrubbery, warily watching dim figures gliding stealthily about and not knowing whether they were friend or foe. Dozens of flares and star shells threw an ethereal, spooky glow along the river and the streets paralleling it. I couldn't find even one of my squad in the dark.

With the dawn, once again, we could identify the enemy. However, the Boche could also identify *us*. I heard a shot ring out close by and a grizzled German ran into the street, blood spurting from a neck wound.

"Kamarad, Kamarad," he screamed.

Just then, another shot sounded and the man's knees buckled, sending him sprawling head long, still yelling in fright. I looked toward the source of the rifle fire. One of the replacements, a boy of sixteen, his face a white mask of terror, fired again and again.

"Stop it!" I shouted. "Stop it, you fool; he's not even armed."

But the kid kept on firing until the man stopped moving.

Sympathy, pity and, at the same time, a sort of horror at the boy's action warred inside me. I looked down at the aged German who reminded me of my father.

Then I thought—as I would again and again during this hellish war—of Lieutenant Robb's admonition that, in war, there were only two kinds of men: the quick and the dead. At least, the young doughboy was still alive, though, I thought, he'd see that aged man's face in his dreams for the rest of his life.

In any case, there was no time to consider the philosophical ramifications of a world that turned a scared kid into a killing machine. A nearby explosion struck the upper story of the house whose shelter I had just left. Incongruously, feathers floated lazily from an upstairs window.

Sergeant Moyer stuck his head out of a doorway just opposite. "That was a potato-masher," he yelled. "Baker, I think we could get a look around from the upstairs on your side."

He darted across the street to join me. Together, we went into the ruined building and climbed what was left of the stairs. From the window, we saw the source of the rifle fire. The Germans appeared to be returning. Some of them were, even now, slipping into the trenches above the town. We alerted the others within hearing distance and opened fire on them. After some time under our concerted fusillade, some sixty of them came out of the trenches, arms above their heads, throwing objects into the bushes.

We secured them in a big barn and left one of my squad, Jimmy Lewis, to guard them. When we advanced to the trenches, which they'd just vacated, we found ten dead Germans and many wounded.

Suddenly, one of the wounded fired at Lieutenant Sanders. The Lieutenant fired back, blowing the man's jaw away with, ironically enough, a German Luger that Sanders had just taken from a prisoner.

The Lieutenant returned to the unwounded prisoners, among whom was a German captain who spoke English. Sanders ordered the officer to accompany him as he went to check on the German wounded our litter-bearers were taking to a dressing station.

A sudden jibbering sound from the soldier whose jaw had been shot away alerted me he was still alive. Nothing was left of the lower half of his face except a shred of tongue. The expression in his blue eyes would have made an angel weep. He looked from my face to the pistol hanging at my belt. His plea was all too eloquent. I tapped it, meeting his tortured gaze. He nodded frantically, making blood flow more freely.

I drew my pistol and tried to aim it, but, God help—or forgive—me, I couldn't pull the trigger. Just then, a sergeant from another company came running toward us.

"Shoot the poor devil," he commanded.

Still, I couldn't. "He could recover . . . ."

The sergeant threw me a furious look. "You damned, yellow-bellied coward," he screamed and, drawing his own pistol, put it to the man's head and pulled the trigger, finishing the poor wretch. "How would *you* like to live like that?" he snarled as he turned away.

We had no time to argue the morality of what was, in essence, the putting down of a human being. All I know is that the sergeant did the merciful thing which I couldn't do; who was the better man? I have carried the picture of that wounded German in my soul all the days of my life.

We herded the rest of the prisoners up onto the bridge back into Fismes, our own stretcher-bearers carrying their wounded, American doughboys helping the less seriously wounded Germans to walk. But, when the German machine gunners in the trenches farther back saw we'd relaxed our guard, they opened fire on their own men —the wounded and the sound—along with their doughboy captors. We couldn't believe our eyes. They were cutting to pieces their own people in order to get the Americans who were trying to help them.

Those of us still on the Fismette side of the river quickly deployed ourselves behind a brick and stone wall that ran along the main street into the town. Lieutenant Thompson ordered us into the cellars of the buildings.

There was no way I was going into the cellars; I'd seen too many instances where houses collapsed, burying men alive. Being Company Gas NCO, I remained behind long enough to post the gas signal before sheltering in the doorway of a building.

Private Frank Waldo of Franklin, Pennsylvania also disobeyed orders. I saw him dragging one of the big German guns to the top story of a house opposite our position. He tore some of the tiles away from the roof, aimed the gun at the Germans' position, and commenced firing. Waldo had much to do with breaking up the German counterattack; when he commenced firing, the enemy's fusillade stopped temporarily as they retreated a bit farther.

I took advantage of this lull in the fighting to investigate the bushes where we'd seen the surrendering Germans dump their belongings. I found three German pistols, one of them longer than usual with rifle sights on the barrel, a half-dozen pocket knives, two watches and a large leather billfold containing the service record of the owner, one Albert Eggers, a letter in German, some postage stamps and some photographs: groups of German soldiers and one of a group of sedate-looking ladies.

The guns, watches, and knives went the way of the other German spoils of war, into the eager hands of Balloon Corps men or other rear-line outfits who didn't have the chance to pick up such souvenirs. I confess our trafficking in German possessions gave me some pangs of conscience. But, I rationalized, the weapons and photographs of our own captured soldiers were being similarly disposed of. Moreover, the Germans had been robbing innocent French civilians as well as Allied soldiers for years.

After the war, I sometimes thought of trying to return Albert Eggers' belongings to Germany through government channels but always drew back from such a course. What if, having set restitution proceedings into motion, Albert Eggers' family learned who I was and wrote to me for information about how I came to have the stuff? What if Albert turned out to be the man with half his face destroyed? Or one of the other wounded, blown off our makeshift bridge along with the American stretcher-bearers who were trying to help them? Perhaps, to Albert Eggers' family, learning *how* he died would be more painful than just learning—from official channels— that he had been killed at Fismette. Finally, I decided to treat the photographs as reverently as I would my own family's and comrades' pictures. And, so, I have Albert Eggers' photos still.

However, as I returned to my doorway, loaded down with German booty, our own artillery, unaware of our presence on this side of the river, suddenly began shelling us. Despite my anxiety about being buried alive, I was forced into the nearest cellar to wait out the barrage.

At last, our own gunners found the right range and aimed their cannon at the enemy. We came out of the cellars to find that Private Waldo was still on the roof, helping the artillery strafe the German lines. The man was a hero, no doubt about it.

As I started to cross the street, a private from Company G fell into step beside me.

"You're from Company F, aren't you?" he asked.

I nodded.

"There's a bunch o' your boys trapped in a cellar down a ways. They need help bad, but I can't stop; got orders to get this dispatch to headquarters, PDQ. See what you can do."

"Sure. And thanks," I said, running off in the direction he'd indicated. In a moment, Corporal Eddie Shoff, also alerted by the dispatch runner, joined me. As we ran along, Sergeant Harry Davis and Private Billy Spyker emerged from a house, carrying a litter with a wounded man on it.

"My God, it's Tom!" yelled Eddie. I saw that it was Corporal Thomas McEwen, Shoff's best friend.

"Put me down a minute, fellows," Tom said, faintly. "I gotta' talk to Eddie."

The stretcher-bearers did as they were asked. McEwen looked up at his friend and said, "There's a can o' corn in my hip pocket, Eddie. It's makin' me uncomfortable. Will you get it out of there?"

Gently, Eddie rolled the Corporal to the side and retrieved the can, setting it on the litter beside him. "I'll come and help you eat it when you get back from the hospital," Eddie said.

McEwen shook his head. "Want you to have it. I got no use for it where I'm goin'," he said. He motioned Davis and Spyker to pick him up and continue towards the river. That was the last we saw him. He died before they reached the comparative safety of Fismes.

A shaken Eddie and I found the cellar where our buddies were trapped and began digging. Others, hearing of the disaster, joined us. When we broke through, we found many wounded: Corporals Jimmy Lewis, Clarence Shaffer, and William Hess of Huntingdon, Sergeant Pat Shields from Franklin, Lewis Engles and some other of the new replacements. I didn't know these men's names and hadn't time just then to inquire what they were and write them down in my diary. There were also fatalities: Privates John Ross and Bert Nail of Franklin, Private First Class James Austin of Edinboro, and Corporal Edward Zuver, of Greenville, who died of his wounds the next day; Privates Allan Lebo of Mohnton, John Cobner of North Braddock, and Thomas Elliot of Pittsburgh, who also died of his wounds the next day, all of whom had been assigned to Company F from the draft pool.

When the stretcher-bearers had removed the wounded and were on their way to the first-aid station near the river, I made my way back to the stone wall where we'd been deployed before the shelling broke out. Others, following general battle instructions, had returned there, too. I plopped down beside Sergeant Cutshall and bugler Private Walter Conrad just as the second wave of German infantry started down the hill. Shortly, Lieutenant Thompson ordered the 1st and 2nd Platoons forward in skirmish formation, through a peach orchard beyond the wall.

My own squad had reconvened and they followed me quickly over the wall and into the orchard. We'd gone but a short distance when Lieutenant Thompson, realizing we were conspicuous targets for the machine-gunning Germans in the topmost trenches, ordered us back to the shelter of the buildings and walls of Fismette. Unfortunately, at the actual command, I was out of earshot of the Lieutenant and didn't hear the order to retreat to the shelter of the town. But, knowing I'd never live to become a hero in the cursed orchard—indeed, I hadn't the chance of a snowball in hell—I dove into the nearest shell hole.

I could hear Sergeant Moyer behind me, directing the fire of the 2nd Platoon. Realizing help was near, I stuck my hand above the rim of the hole and waved, praying the German sharpshooters wouldn't pick me off like a turkey at a shoot.

"Flocko, it's me, Zeb," I yelled. I'm in a small hole 'bout a hundred yards from the wall. Can you cover me until I get back?"

However, I was too damned scared to wait for an answer; I scrambled out of the hole and dashed toward the wall, running erratically to confound their aims. When the Germans saw me, they really opened fire. I'd almost reached the wall when I stumbled over a root and went down.

"They got ol' Zebbie," Flocko bellowed.

"The hell they did," I yelled, already back on my feet and racing for the shelter of the wall. Many willing hands pulled me over to safety.

I looked around, failing to see the bugler who'd gone over with us. "Where's Walt?" I asked.

"Shot through the arm, Zeb. Lieutenant sent him to the first-aid station. He'll be okay." The Sergeant looked solemn. "You lost one o' your squad, though, Zeb. He got shot through the head as he followed you through the peach orchard."

"No. Which one?" I asked, my heart feeling like a grapefruit in my throat.

"That Italian kid from Mapleton, young Joe DeMario. His buddy, Private Frank Cristini . . . and Corporal Harry Johnson from Franklin. Corporal Charles Dunkle from Clarendon wounded. Damned near got you, too."

"Yeah, I noticed."

He grunted and picked up his gun. "I think the Lieutenant made a big mistake orderin' us forward on that one," he added.

We settled down behind the wall and began returning the enemy fire. How they could possibly be hammering us so badly, considering the losses they'd received, is a mystery I still haven't figured out. The hellish shelling continued long after dark. During that time, Company F and Company H never budged an inch from where they had us pinned down, though we were bone weary and had eaten nothing all day.

Toward midnight, Ernie and I had fallen into an exhausted sleep when, suddenly, we were shaken awake by little Billy Spyker.

"Come on, you guys, you gotta get outta here," he said urgently. "The Lieutenant ordered the 112th to retreat across the river to Fismes. When I realized you two weren't with us, I figured you must not have heard the command."

Ernie and I exchanged glances. "So you took the chance to come for us," Ernie said gratefully. "You're a regular little hero, Billy."

Billy threw us his lighthearted grin. "Ah, no. I just knew you hadn't heard. Didn't want you two to be caught when the Germans retake Fismette."

I clapped him on the back, too moved to speak. The happy kid from Alexandria, Pennsylvania had been scrounging in the dark all night for ammunition, taking it from fallen soldiers' ammo belts, even wading back across the wire-littered river in the dark to fetch it for us.

We ran quickly across the bridge in the dark, the Germans moving to retake Fismette right on our heels, and rejoined our outfit.

Lieutenant Thompson had established his post of command in a house not too badly damaged by shellfire. He welcomed us with a relieved smile and shook our hands.

We joined the line of doughboys filling their canteens at the beautiful fountain in the middle of the town square which we'd dared not approach during daylight. The enemy still had the range of the fountain, however, and I had just reached it when their artillery barrage started again. The jet of water, perpetually shooting six feet into the air, was joined by another as a shell hit the fountain. All of us near the fountain were knocked to the ground. But, we were still alive.

In the morning, our replacements having arrived, we were ordered back to Fond de Mezieres, the place we'd dubbed Death Valley, dodging German gunfire all the way. Private First Class Floyd Krepps was hit in the leg. When some of us dropped back to assist him, we found Lieutenant Sanders was there before us.

"Keep going, boys," he said. "I'll help him."

We obeyed. Later, we learned he'd pulled Krepps to the side of the road and dressed his wound, staying with him until an ambulance could come to rescue them. Was it any wonder our admiration for the little officer from New York state kept growing? I think he was one of the finest officers in the AEF.

Breakfast and water to clean ourselves up a little was waiting at Death Valley before we crawled into our bedrolls and fell asleep.

We were soon awakened when our officers ordered us back a bit to a smaller valley because the artillerymen complained that our presence was drawing excessive enemy fire. In the comparative safety of this little valley, we learned the losses the 112th had sustained during the day and night at Fismette.

Private Wilbur Corbin, another boy from my squad, wounded in the back and thigh; Private Bob Rickleton of Franklin, shoulder wound; Corporal Ed Griffith, a replacement from Iowa, shoulder and side wound; Privates William Cotterman of Tidioute, Abe Smith of Kennerdell, and Emil Pashley of Franklin, bullet wounds to their bodies; Private Albert Minnich of Palmyra, another of my squad members, bullet wound to the head; Private George Godard of Huntingdon, gassed.

Those wounded during the afternoon skirmish in the peach orchard were Private First Class Frank Harvey, bullet through the cheek, later resulting in the loss of an eye; Private First Class Chuck Anderson, wounded; and our own Sergeant Cutshall who'd taken a bullet through the elbow as he lay beside me behind that everlasting wall. All afternoon and evening, he'd kept shooting at the enemy. And never once mentioned his wound until after the retreat to Fismes.

CHAPTER 7

Wipe-out of Companies G and H

The attempt to take Fismes and Fismette cost the Allies dearly. Our own regiment was no exception. The official list of casualties for the 112th up until August 9, when we were relieved by the 111th, included 12 officers and 396 enlisted men: 41 killed, 168 wounded, 128 gassed, and 59 missing. The force remaining consisted of 67 officers and 2,763 enlisted men.

We were sent to rest behind the lines near Dravagny where regimental headquarters had been established at the edge of town farthest from the front. The 2nd Battalion and the machine-gun company were ordered to take up defensive positions near Longville; the 1st Battalion at Fond de Gloriette.

The retreat from the front commenced at 4 AM. Puss Hawn and I, who'd started the march side by side, became separated from the company and, a few minutes later, from each other, because of the dense fog. We dared not call out in the choking stuff since we had no idea where the Germans might be; there were reports of them having broken through the 111th lines at some points, reaching our side of the river.

For some time, I kept moving, probably in a circle, an eerie sense of isolation nearly unmanning me. I was more frightened than I'd been in Fismette where I could at least see the German gunners. Then, realizing I'd never get my bearings until the fog lifted, likely at dawn, I sat down with my back against a stack of cordwood some farmer had placed there, prepared to wait for daylight.

Suddenly, I heard someone moving across the cut-over field. I jumped to my feet, my bayonet at the ready. The sound of movement was so loud in the heavy air that I thought it might well have been a cow or horse lumbering through the dark, but a few muttered curses—*doughboy* curses—in a voice I recognized dispelled that idea. I smiled and lowered my rifle; it was ol' Puss.

I called out softly to him and, in a moment, his sheepish, familiar grin emerged from the fog. Sagging with relief, I laid my rifle atop the woodpile and sat down again.

"I got almost to the river. Never caught sight nor sound o' the company. No Fritzies, either, for that matter," he muttered as he leaned his rifle against the woodpile and sat down beside me.

We could hear shooting in the distance near the river. The fog looked as thick as the stew-like concoction called slum-gullion which the cooks served up by the vatful.

"Well, I said, "no point in trying to find the others until daylight; may as well get a little shut-eye."

"Naw, Zebbie, I ain't sleepin' in this fog," Puss said. "I know how to get to a better place." He rose and picked up his rifle. "Come on, stay close."

I took my rifle and, treading almost on his heels, followed him. He led me to a huge tree which had been literally uprooted by shellfire, leaving a pit where its roots had been. They loomed above us, a bare shade darker than the foggy night.

"Watch your step, Zeb, the sides o' the hole are kinda' slick with mud."

I peered through the exposed roots and saw that he was right.

"Careful climbin' in. It's a little drier and a whole lot safer in there than it is out here," Puss said, dropping out of sight.

I climbed in behind him, brushing the slithery roots away from my face.

I could hear—and vaguely see—Puss as he spread his poncho on the ground. Then he said. "Use yours to cover us."

"I don't know, Puss, it stinks something awful in here," I said doubtfully.

He snorted in doughboy derision. "You're gettin' awful damned dainty all of a sudden. What d'you expect from a hole in the ground? At least we'll be dry and we won't get hit with a shell."

He had a point there, so, trying to ignore the smell, I stretched out in the dark beside him, resting my head on a soft clump of earth, and pulled my side of the poncho over me.

I awakened in the first misty light of dawn, nearly gagging from the odor, now worse than ever in this closed space, but, not wanting to awaken Puss who was snoring peacefully, I lay still, looking up through the roots above me for the dawn. As the light strengthened, I realized with horror the source of the awful odor. Draped across the roots of the tree like Spanish moss was human viscera. *That*, not wet roots, had been what had brushed against my face.

I reared up and shook Puss violently. As I did so, I saw that my erstwhile pillow was a dismembered human thigh, with traces of a German gray-green uniform plastered to it by blood.

When Puss saw the macabre draperies of our bed, even his cast-iron stomach rebelled. Perpetually hungry as we were, had we been served the finest steak dinner the Waldorf-Astoria Hotel had to offer, we'd have refused it. We scrambled out of the hole and, in the strengthening light, set out to find the rest of our company.

Others, too, had been lost in the fog, but, eventually, we reassembled, only to discover the expected order to relieve the beleaguered 111th hadn't yet reached Lieutenant Thompson.

So, again, we were told to hurry up and wait which, in this instance, included digging trenches for ourselves in a wooded area a few miles from Dravagny. Here, on Saturday, August 17, a contingent of draftees from Camp Lee, Virginia arrived by truck to replace the men we'd lost in battle. Needless to say, this boosted our morale considerably, but not nearly as much as our next order did.

The entire company was told to fall in and march to an old chocolate factory near the town of Annaye d'Igny where a bathhouse of sorts had been rigged. Each filthy, lousy doughboy got to take a hot bath with lots of soap, the first in a long time. We even got new clothing, as long as the limited supply lasted. I doubt heaven can possibly feel any better than getting out of our lousy underwear and into clean new suits. Our elation didn't last long, though, since few among us got *all* new clothing. There was enough breeding stock in our old puttees, jackets or trousers to start a new generation of cooties overnight.

We relieved the 111th on the night of August 18–19. Colonel George Rickards ordered the company commanders to take only able-bodied men, saying a hundred good men to a company was better than a full complement of men who could get in the way of action. The wounded would only hinder us, he said. The order also expressed his worry about the absence of enemy fire and cautioned his officers to see that the men stayed strictly out of sight and, especially, that we not gather in groups, easy targets for the enemy artillery.

Companies A and C took over Fismette; B Company was assigned the right flank on the Fismes side of the river, part of Company D on the left flank. The 1st Battalion of the 28th was next and, just behind, the 308th Infantry of the 77th Division to the left, the 110th Regiment of the 55th Brigade to the right. The 2nd Battalion—Company F's—had the support position a little south of St. Giles and the 3rd Battalion was stationed one kilometer west of St. Giles.

On the night of the 22nd, the 3rd Battalion received orders to relieve the 1st Battalion. On August 23, Company A extended the line to the left of Fismette, but, at the same time, reports came through that the Germans had recaptured the eastern section of Fismes. If my account sounds confused, please remember that this rain and fog-enshrouded battle for the Vesle River was so erratic that it wasn't correctly chronicled for months. During the actual August battle, it was difficult to know which side of the Vesle the opposing forces occupied at any given time. The Germans at the Fismes/Fismette sector proved to be much stronger than the Allies had supposed. And, of course, knowing the war was inexorably turning against them with America now completely involved, they fought with all the fury of animals defending their very lives.

It was during this night that Companies G and H of the 112th, except for 6 enlisted men and 2 lieutenants, were wiped out. The survivors had to swim the barbed-wire littered Vesle to escape. They said the Germans had swarmed into the town in a great horde, perhaps a thousand of them. Officers who heard their story didn't credit it at the time. The complete story of the massacre of Companies G and H on the Vesle only came out much later when Lieutenants Schmelzer, Fredenburgh, and Young, who'd been captured, were released from German prison camps after the war ended and told what had happened. The two units had sustained casualties of 60 to 70 killed, 51 wounded and taken prisoner, and 88 non-wounded taken prisoner. Among the officers killed was Lieutenant Landry, a popular rifle instructor at Camp Hancock.

Since most companies in the Great War were originally volunteers from the same town, I couldn't imagine the devastation on G and H companies' home towns. I couldn't help thinking how horrible it would be for any small town—for Huntingdon—to have lost most of her young men in one battle.

There was no doubt about it; the Germans had poured everything they had into the battle for the Vesle River. Certainly, the numbers of the enemy seemed inexhaustible to us Company F boys as we lay behind the stone wall that night in front of the peach orchard and shot at them.

The enemy shock troops who had defended Fismette numbered a thousand hand-picked men, greatly outnumbering us. The loss of G and H put Company F in a somewhat precarious position, especially as we'd lost contact with the French Division that had been on our right flank. Our only protection from surprise attacks was to keep our patrols out at night to warn us in time. Major Phelps had been wounded again and taken to the rear. Major Smathers, returning from Cichy where he'd been treated for a severe gassing during the first battle of Fismes/Fismette, replaced him and immediately restored order.

To this day, I cannot understand why there was not more effective liaison between the divisions on this critical front. Perhaps it was just the incompetence that seems to plague all human endeavors. Maybe officers, as human as the men they command, do stupid things under fire. Fact is, *all* wars are just plain stupid. If I had my way, the ones who cause them would have to fight them.

Thank heaven, during this second deployment at the Fisme sector, Company F, being held more or less in reserve near St. Giles, managed to hold its own without too many further casualties.

But, on the night of August 28, we were ordered to advance under a barrage laid down by our own artillery to a position along a high railroad embankment below the dam of the Vesle. The Allies now held the railroad. Control of it—for the moving of men and arms—made this sector of vital importance to both sides. The section we drew to defend was extremely vulnerable, with no cover whatsoever. We lay at the base of the steep rail-road embankment, in plain view of the German observation balloon that systematically moved back and forth across the area. The only accessible water was a small spring a few hundred yards down the track at the edge of a copse of trees.

At night, two of our number took turns making trips to the spring, holding a long stick between them on which they could carry many can-teens. However, the Germans, knowing of the spring's existence, kept up a steady barrage from their light field guns all around the spring, throughout the night, so that fetching water became a deadly roulette game.

Under cover of the darkness, Private Jim Weir hauled our heavy Chauchat to the top of the embankment and a couple of squads of riflemen made it, too.

The rest of us clung to the bank, our rifles trained on the Germans farther from the tracks; the railroad had to be held at all costs. We could hear their engineers working on a bridge across the river.

Suddenly, a bigger shell than usual hit a heavy switch lever above us, tearing it loose from its moorings and hurling it down the bank. It raised a small avalanche of cinders, which quickly buried Private Fred Flake and Private Awkie Beck. Puss Hawn, who could be counted on for effective action in most contingencies, saw his little friend, Awkie, disappear in the black cloud and, pulling the long-handled shovel he always carried from his pack, scrambled toward the place where they'd disappeared, the rest of us on his heels. He began to dig frantically with his shovel in the black cinders, the rest of us with our hands. We pulled Fred out, unhurt except for a little concussion, but when we finally reached poor little Awkie, he was dead. There wasn't a mark on him; he'd suffocated in the cinders. Big Puss, tears making tracks in his dirty face, carried Awkie down the embankment, away from the cinders that had killed him, and dug a grave for his friend in clean soil, a few feet away from the embankment.

This unusual activity in our line attracted the attention of the Ger-mans. We heard their approach and Sergeant Frederick Burford ordered us to move as quietly as possible up the embankment and on to the tracks. From that vantage point, we watched as they reached our just-vacated position. At the same time, a second German patrol came slipping silently along the embankment from the other direction. Mistaking each other for us, they opened fire and many men fell.

Sergeant Burford used this opportunity to attack those still standing.

"Open fire!" he thundered and we followed him down the embank-ment, quickly routing the survivors of their own blunder. They took off run-ning and, a few minutes later, perhaps overestimating our strength be-cause of the way we thundered down on them from above, they blew up their own bridge so we couldn't pursue them.

Our jubilation didn't make up for losing Awkie, but it helped. I hoped he knew that his funeral had been the reason they'd made the blunder that helped us hold the railroad.

After losing two entire companies, Major Miller and Major Smathers organized a picked provisional force comprised of the most experienced men of the 56th Brigade who would head a massive drive to oust the enemy from Fismette once and for all. But, before they could put their plan into action, word came down from Regimental P.C. that the 28th Division would be relieved on September 8 and 9. Major Miller, while still a captain, in the July 24th battle at Chateau-Thierry, had taken five shrapnel wounds that had been expected to kill him. He'd recovered and been promoted to major.

One evening, Ross Thompson—recently promoted to captain—sent a runner to summon me to Company P.C. a few yards back of the firing lane. I left my post at once and reported.

Captain Thompson looked up when I reached him.

"In about five minutes, I want you to guide a Battalion of the 80th Division to the front," he said, showing me on the map where I'd find them. "Warn the commanders in advance that there is to be no smoking or talking. Tell them to avoid the garbage dump back of this sector; it'd be noisy if they blunder into that. They are to advance single file, putting their feet directly where *you* trod. Tell them to obey implicitly."

"Yes, Sir," I said and saluted. I don't mind admitting I was proud to be entrusted with such a commission.

"Good luck, Corporal," he said.

I found the battalion quickly where the Captain had indicated on the map. I was totally unprepared for the inexperience, indeed, the hilarity of the brand-new doughboys. Their young officer didn't look much older than they were and he returned my salute lazily. The men were shouting and singing, some were even drinking. The din was so great, I couldn't make myself heard when I tried to convey the Captain's orders. At last, by shouting myself and making motions, I convinced him to command silence.

He turned to me and said, "Are you an officer?"

"No, Sir, just a corporal."

"And we're supposed to listen to you?"

"Captain Thompson trusted me enough to lead you to your position, Sir. He made a point of telling me to caution you in the strongest manner possible that there must be absolute quiet in the ranks unless you want to get blown away by German gunfire." The new soldiers all began babbling at once. I raised my voice a little and looked at them. "*I* don't want to get blown away; do you?"

That finally got through to their officer who gave them merry hell. Then he turned to me and said, "Are you sure you know where to take us?"

"Yes, Sir. But please tell your men they are to walk single file, each man stepping in the tracks of the man ahead of him. There's a garbage dump we must avoid. Anyone who stumbles into that will raise so much noise they'll hear us in Berlin. Do you understand?"

He said he did and the young soldiers all nodded. We marched into the night, lit only by the flares in the sky above. The sound of the guns, now that we'd left headquarters, sobered them at last. Nevertheless, one of the inebriated oafs managed to blunder off the narrow track and into the dump which was full of rusted junk and cans and bottles. Gone was all possibility of keeping our approach quiet. There was nothing for it but to race to the safety of the trenches ahead before the Jerries turned their guns on the source of the noise.

"Keep moving, don't stop," I yelled and raced for the trenches.

With all the finesse of a herd of cattle, they obeyed me. Jumping into the trenches beside the men they were to replace, they started firing—without so much as aiming—at the enemy line.

Sergeant Burford's voice began blistering their ears. "What's the matter with you? You all nit-wits?" he roared. "Settle down or you'll get your damned heads blown off." Then he called down the line. "You fellows from Company F get the hell outta here. If you can, now that these clowns have stirred up Fritzies' hive. I'll be along soon's I get them settled down a bit."

We needed little urging.

However, as we climbed out of the trenches on our bellies and started to the rear, we realized the new men's shooting had attracted the artillery fire to the front trench, not to us. Most of the shells were falling there. I shook my head as I crawled away, saying a prayer for the new recruits . . . and for Sergeant Burford.

CHAPTER 8

Advance to the Argonne Forest

We arrived at our new billeting area near Death Valley late in the afternoon. Our Field Kitchen unit was already there, the cooks waiting to serve us supper. Needless to say, we did it justice.

The next morning, we were off again, marching in the pouring rain. Leaving the Fismes/Fismette sector felt like stopping before a job was properly finished, but our officers decided to save the 112th for what would surely be the climax of the war. And it was coming fast. Colonel Rickards had been put in charge of the 56th Brigade, while Major Smathers took over command of the 112th.

We'd been exposed to the possibility—and, often, the actuality—of enemy fire for weeks on end, so, mingled with our disappointment at leaving a battle before its conclusion, was relief that we were actually headed away from the hellish front. Despite the downpour, our spirits lifted as we marched. We hadn't the least idea where we were going, but it was away from the front and that was enough.

We hiked down the Marne Valley. In a day and a half's march, we covered over 32 miles in the rain, arriving at the wine-producing town of Epernay late the following day. Here, we climbed into trucks—sixteen men and equipment to each—and were driven, through the beautiful countryside near Chalons-sur-Marne, to the town of Blesme-Haussignnemont, arriving on September 13.

By now, the French poilus in their bright blue uniforms had taken to calling the 28th the Iron Division as Pershing himself dubbed us. As complimentary as the moniker was, in a way, the Germans' name for us was even more flattering. Recognizing our red keystone insignias, they referred to us as the bucket of blood division, saying our emblems looked like buckets full of the German blood we had drawn.

But as we marched, clothes and packs soaked, we didn't feel like fierce warriors; we were just a bunch of homesick doughboys, sickened by the blood we'd shed and the friends we'd lost.

At the end of another seven kilometers' march, we arrived in Maurupt le Montoy, one of the hillside towns above the Marne from which the Germans had been driven earlier in the summer. The rain stopped just as we entered the town. The citizens had returned to their homes and, despite their severely limited stock, shopkeepers were doing a brisk business with the merchandise they'd acquired while exiled to near Chateau-Thierry when the Germans had occupied the town. The whistle of a nearby locomotive added a strangely comforting and mundane sound to the peaceful surroundings.

We bivouacked on a hillside, gratefully dropping our drenched packs and cartridge belts. I caught a glimpse of an unattended provision wagon down the road a bit, so, being a skinny guy, always hungry, I left my possessions to dry without me and went to see what it might provide in the way of belly fodder. Moseying idly by, I snatched a can of what I took to be peaches, which I love, and stuffed them into my jacket. I ambled back to camp where I discovered some low-down thief had stolen my nice, shiny 45 automatic pistol and replaced it with a rusty wreck of a 45. To add insult to injury, when I plopped down and reached for my knife to open the can, I discovered I'd swiped a can of tomatoes, which I loathe, instead of peaches.

Well, I thought ruefully, my mother had tried to teach me that crime doesn't pay. But it sure did for the guy who took my 45.

The two peaceful days we spent there enabled us to get cleaned up and spend some of our accumulated three months' pay, in my case, after the amount the army sent home, a little over thirty dollars.

When I got home from France, I found that I'd lost the notes for some of these days and must credit my friend, Bob Appleby, who was a greater fanatic than I was about keeping a written account of our war experiences.

Bob was somewhat older than most of us when he enlisted in 1916. The son of a Civil War veteran, he was married with half-grown children at home. He could easily have been mustered out in Georgia before Company F left for France, but disdained to take advantage of his status. He had a profound sense of duty to his country and obligation to stop the depredations of the Hun against most of the countries of Europe. Time after time, Bob turned down promotions, saying he preferred being just "one of the boys." I often felt there was more to it than that; he hated the trappings of command. A fatherly man, I have often seen him staggering under the weight of his own pack and that of some weary kid who was faltering in the march. On the battlefield, he would ignore his own safety to go out and help some wounded soldier. He seemed almost *compelled* to compassion. Casual in dress, happy-faced, born to serve, that was Bob Appleby. Later, as a civilian, he served his community as faithfully as he had Company F; he was elected again and again to the post of prothonotary of Huntingdon County.

We had reached Sermaise-sur-Baines when the division's wagon train caught up to us, bearing news that General Pershing and his shock divisions had wiped out the St.-Mihiel salient. This was the only major engagement of the war—since America's entry into it—that the 28th Division took no part in.

To say there was jubilation at this great coup in our temporary barracks would be an understatement. We couldn't have been in a better area to celebrate either than here where they made such fine wine and champagne and offered it for sale in the ubiquitous estaminets.

We returned to the inevitable drilling and parted with the last of our money in the shops. I bought a small copper-tone brooch with "Sermaise" soldered across the top which I sent home to my mother.

We left Sermaise on the evening of Monday, September 16, supposedly to march to Verdun.

"We're not going to Verdun," Bob Appleby declared as we marched. "We're taking the shortest route to Jerry's fatherland."

"Where's that?" several boys asked.

"The Argonne Forest," he replied. "It's only logical. We've got 'em on the run; we'll chase them clear to Germany."

He was right. And thereby proved my opinion that he ought to have been a general.

We hiked for several days, the packs growing ever heavier. The replacements we'd received after losing so many at Fismette seemed to have the makings of fair soldiers; at least they were keeping up with us old-timers.

Weeks before, my cousin, Harry "Tony" Maier, had picked up an iron skillet, of all things, and carried it strapped on the top of his pack. The fellows had begun kidding him, saying he had to be crazy adding the weight of an iron skillet to his heavy pack. Indeed, hauling the skillet had earned him the nickname "Mad Ike." The packs were so heavy that we left behind anything not essential to life and anyone who would voluntarily tote an *iron skillet* was, justifiably, deemed crazy.

Family honor demanded I try to talk him out of his craziness.

"Tony, the skillet's breaking your back," I pointed out. "Drop the damned thing."

"Might come in handy," he replied stubbornly.

As we marched through a good-sized town late one afternoon, the order came to fall out for a rest. I plopped down and began filling my pipe. Tony unstrapped his pack and freed the skillet. He pried two bricks out of the roadway and, as nonchalantly as if he were in my aunt's kitchen back home, he set the skillet atop them and began building a little fire of branches and twigs under it. By now, doughboys were crowding around, hooting with laughter at Mad Ike's antics. Ignoring them, Tony unrolled his bedroll to reveal a large hen's egg which he'd picked up somewhere on the march. Miraculously, it hadn't broken.

He broke the egg into the hot skillet and scrambled it with his fork, blissfully unmindful of his audience.

"Where d'ya learn to cook, Tony?" one boy jibed.

"Ya gonna eat the whole thing yourself, Tony?" another asked wistfully.

"How 'bout a taste, Mad Ike?"

But like the little red hen, Tony had endured everyone's ridicule for weeks and, also like the little red hen, he intended to eat it all himself. So he slowly swallowed the last morsel, cleaned his skillet with a handful of sod, replaced the bricks in the roadway, strapped his skillet to the top of his pack, and fell back into the line of march.

Some 30,000 doughboys undertook that forced march and, inevitably, there were stragglers. But the officers didn't seem much concerned about desertions and, when we reached the Argonne Forest, their faith was justified. Of course, desertions from the AEF were always negligible; after all, their *was* an ocean between the Americans and their home.

We bivouacked at the edge of the woods near Le Nefour to wait for the others. It took two days for everyone to join us, but in they came, sometimes whole companies together. By the time we were ordered into the woods for some further drilling and a refresher course in map reading, fewer than a dozen had failed to catch up.

During the wait, I spent the evenings walking about in the beautiful forest. On my way back to camp one evening, I was startled to hear a chuckle coming from behind a tin-roofed shed. Stopping to investigate, I found Carl "Poogey" Coffman, a little private from F company, stripped to the waist and "reading" his shirt which was suspended from a peg above him. Reading one's shirt was doughboy jargon for picking vermin from it. And, boy, did Poogey ever have reading matter! His shirt appeared to be literally crawling, undulating, rippling with movement.

"What's funny about cooties, Poogey?" I asked.

"*They* ain't funny. But, I was just sittin' here thinkin' those damned cooties are sure gonna' be surprised tonight when they go lookin' for Poogey to bite and he ain't there. *That's* funny." And, still chuckling, he stalked off into the woods for a night's sleep without the company of his tiny friends.

During the week of September 20, preparations for the great Argonne offensive moved rapidly forward. The biggest guns we'd yet seen, long-barreled coast-defense guns, painted in camouflage and requiring tractors to move them, were being loaded onto railroad cars to be transported to the front. Thousands of trucks, groaning under their burdens of artillery shells, began pouring through the forest.

At last, the 56th Brigade moved stealthily through the night to the jumping off point for relieving the French holding Appremont and Varrenes. The great forest effectively concealed all the Allies' movements, being impenetrable to the observers in balloons, or to the rays of the sun for that matter. Smoking or showing oneself at the edge of the forest was strictly forbidden and, almost miraculously, the vast movement of men and machines through the forest went undetected by the Germans.

The French had managed to hold on to only a small part of the forest through the years and at a staggering cost in lives. Here, the trench system was more extensive than anything we'd seen, going on for miles with hundred-yard wide belts of barbed wire stretched out in front of the trenches, even concrete bunkers here and there. Dugouts dotted the hillsides and, beyond this bastion, lay a battleground that even the intrepid French said could never be taken by a direct frontal attack.

They didn't know General Pershing and the AEF. On September 21, Lieutenant Colonel John Bubb of the regular army took over command of the regiment from Major Smathers until October 3 when command was given to Lieutenant Colonel James Shannon.

On the night of September 25, we lay down to sleep, still secure in the knowledge that the enemy had not yet learned of our presence in the French part of the forest. We were awakened about midnight to all hell breaking loose; our own artillery had commenced the battle without bothering to warn us. Some of the new recruits got the wind up temporarily but soon quieted down. I must confess, even us old vets of the Marne and Vesle campaigns were rattled by the suddenness of the assault.

With alacrity we obeyed the order to gather our equipment and fall in. The roadway was jammed with wagons and trucks, still hauling ammunition to the front, while the French we were relieving tried to make their way to the rear. We had to stop frequently to help the mules and horses pull the wagons free of boggy places in the rain-drenched roads or clear away tangles of barbed wire. At one point, in order to continue our march to the front, we had to, literally, duck under the long-barreled guns as they blazed away. It's a miracle any of us had intact eardrums, not to mention our courage, after that night. Indeed, it was while we were crawling along beneath the guns that a new recruit suddenly threw down his rifle and ran, screaming back the way we'd come.

"Grab that yellow son-of-a-bitch," I heard his sergeant roar.

A truck driver jammed on his brakes to avoid hitting the kid and an officer, sitting beside the driver jumped out and took the boy by the arms.

"As you were, Sergeant," he yelled above the din. "I'll see that he gets to the hospital."

I had to keep moving and didn't see what happened. God knows, the kid was only giving way to the impulse we all shared. I think even the sergeant who expressed such contempt for the boy, was doing so to squelch his own fear demon.

The 2nd Battalion reached the front sometime after midnight. We lay under cover until daylight, watching our artillery shells exploding, occasionally hitting a German ammunition pile with spectacular results. I was munching on a piece of French hardtack, waiting for the second barrage to ease when the order to go over the top came.

"All right, let's go," shouted our Captain and the battle of the Argonne began in earnest for the boys from Huntingdon.

After that first charge, to our amazement, not one German gun was fired; they'd been blasted to smithereens by our artillery. And the first line of the German infantry had been destroyed as well. We advanced rapidly through the shell-pocked terrain, dodging barbed wire barriers, covering about 8 kilos before we came smack against more machine-gun and rifle fire. Late in the afternoon, amidst a driving rain, we dug into a hillside and settled into the now familiar hole-in-the-ground combat.

During the night, an elderly German soldier blundered into our position. When we took him prisoner, he was so delighted not to be shot that he answered all our questions, even volunteering some information we hadn't asked for, and accompanied Major Miller and a detachment of riflemen to point out his own outfit. Without his information, when daylight came, our entire sector would have been caught in a cross fire from machine guns and a scattering of pillboxes on the next hill. I've no doubt the old boy wasn't so much concerned with *our* safety as with his own, but, nevertheless, his information prompted Colonel Rickards to order an immediate withdrawal so that our artillery could clean out the deadly nests.

Once again, I nearly got trapped into a situation where I could be hit by our own artillery as I'd been at Fismette when Billy Spyker saved me and Ernie Cutshall. Private First Class Jack Buffett of Philadelphia and I had crawled into a pit to escape the rifle-fire and, fairly effectively pinned down, gave up and fell asleep. Jack's brother, Roland, missed Jack after Colonel Rickards' order and came searching for him, probably saving our lives.

However, dawn came before we were all safely withdrawn from our perilous position. The last of our force made for the ridge behind us amidst German gunfire. Once out of range, we were relieved by the 111th and we went, gratefully, back to the camp kitchens for a hot meal, the first in many days.

During this respite, our artillery laid down a deadly barrage which did much to remove the danger to the infantry and the 111th advanced to our former position at the crest of Le Chene Tondu ridge. After we'd finished our meal, we fell in and retraced our steps for the two miles to come to the aid of the 111th. They'd dug into our former position but reaching them wasn't so easy. Now, we had to outflank them to avoid the line of fire. For two hours, we struggled through trees shattered by the artillery barrage and nigh impenetrable barbed-wire barriers. We finally arrived at another ridge facing the right slope of Le Chene Tondu which was preventing a clean sweep to the cliffs of Chatel Chehery. Beyond that point lay miles of open country which, heretofore, had proved disasterous to the enemy.

Our advance up this hillside proved torturous, hampered at every hesitant step by enemy machine-gun fire. Company F finally reached the top at about dark without losing one man, but other companies weren't so lucky. Indeed, the 111th, which had relieved us so we could get a meal, had sustained heavy losses in the first advance after the artillery barrage. For this day at least, the fortunes of war had favored Company F.

During that night, Lieutenant Burdick called out softly to Corporal Aiken and me as we lay in a gully near his position.

"Tell the Captain I'm returning to the wagons to get some dry socks," he said.

Aiken looked at me. Corporals *didn't* argue with lieutenants. Nevertheless, gathering his courage, he said, "Please don't take a chance, Sir. I've got an extra pair of socks in my pack you can have."

"Thanks, Corporal," came the reply. "But I'm low on ammo, too. I'll be okay. See you in the morning."

We didn't. The sound of his stealthy progress back down the hill was the last we ever heard of him. He turned up after the war, having been gassed and gone to the hospital.

The advance from this position started at daybreak. The Germans on the opposing crest had prudently retreated during the night. We pushed on into the forest, encountering so much barbed wire that, often, we had to circle back and leapfrog through the 111th line, ousting the Germans we encountered with hand grenades and bayonets.

This maneuver went on for days of intense, often hand-to-hand combat, but at last, we advanced to a little clearing in the forest where some farmer had planted a garden. The wonder of finding growing, living things in the midst of death and destruction was an unexpected delight. Several of us, including Sergeant James Richey of Franklin and Billy Spyker stopped to gather some of the fat cabbages.

"Boy-o-boy, Zeb, will these taste good," Billy said, beaming like a kid with an all-day sucker.

Suddenly, the rat-a-tat of machine-gun fire broke the silence. I dropped the cabbage I was holding and turned to run for cover, just as a bullet took Billy in the neck.

Sergeant Richey and I grabbed the little guy between us and made for the shelter of the trees as the vicious gunfire pursued us. Richey took a bullet in the foot and we would, surely, have been killed had not Corporal Bob White of Franklin come through the trees at that moment, sized up the situation, and shot the gunner whose position in the tree was perfect for ambushing raiders of the garden. Only his gunfire alerted White to his position.

As the man slumped and would have fallen, we saw for ourselves that what we'd been told about the Germans chaining their rear guard gunners to trees so they couldn't flee was true; he hung there, dead, in his chains.

Stretcher-bearers came quickly and took Billy and James to the rear for treatment. When, later that day, I heard that Billy had died, I admit I shed some damned unsoldierly tears. If it hadn't been for Billy that night at Fismes, Ernie and I would long since have "gone west." I thought of the little fellow's sunny smile and pleasing disposition and the love that would prompt such sacrifice in a man, and I cursed this vicious war. I knew I couldn't have felt worse had he been my own little brother, Charlie. His action at Fismes was one of the many unheralded acts of bravery during the war.

When it was all over, Billy's hometown of Alexandria, Pennsylvania, which lay a few miles west of Huntingdon, honored him by naming the American Legion Post after him, the first boy from the little town killed in the Great War. The day it was announced, I fancied he knew. I kept seeing his happy grin in my heart's eye. I was alive to applaud the honor bestowed on him because of his bravery. Indeed, many years later, Sergeant Cutshall's grandson married my granddaughter. Neither would have been born except for Billy. The day they married, I couldn't help but think of the brave little fellow from Alexandria. How I wished I had been able to save *him*.

But, on the day Alexandria honored her hero soldier/son, I could only recite to myself the poem I'd written for Billy in France, scrawling it in my notebook the first chance I got.

> How can we e'er forget him,
> Our comrade loyal and true,
> Who shared our every danger,
> 'Neath the red, the white and the blue.
>
> He was reckless, brave and smiling,
> Never did he once complain,
> But he used to cheer us all along,
> As we plodded through dark and rain.
>
> He always aided a comrade,
> Stricken on the firing line,
> And if you asked him for a favor,
> You'd get it every time.
>
> But one bright and sunny noontime,
> Emerging from the forest's gloom,
> A rifle cracked, a bullet whined,
> And our comrade met his doom.
>
> The same cheerful smile was on his face,
> No bitterness shone through,
> And his memory we'll always cherish,
> It's all that we can do.
>
> For him, our loyal comrade,
> Who fell 'neath the red, white and blue.

CHAPTER 9

No-Man's-Land

We dug in to hold our hard-won line, piling dirt before our improvised trenches as a sort of bulwark. About midnight, a runner from Battalion P.C. came up to our position with a message for all company commanders that read: "Be prepared to attack at once. No further orders forthcoming or needed."

The Captain, who'd received the order sitting in the trench near Puss Hawn and me, let his breath out in a whoosh. "This sounds ominous. And fishy. Have either of you boys seen Corporal Snyder?"

Buddy Snyder of Franklin was our company runner. Neither Puss nor I had seen him and said so.

"Baker, do you know how to find Battalion P.C. in the dark?"

"Yes, Sir, I can. It's not far."

"Then go find Major Miller to confirm this order. Get back to me as quick as you can."

I reached for my pack.

"No, leave your pack here. Take only your 45, cartridge belt and rifle. I want you traveling light and fast."

I set out into a night as black as the inside of a camera. It wasn't long until Snyder caught up with me. Dark as it was, experienced as Snyder was, we soon lost our way. I fell into a trench that shouldn't have been there and Snyder fell on top of me, knocking the wind out of me with the full force of his hobnailed boots in the small of my back. We crawled out of the trench, more cautiously now, and ranged around until we found someone to direct us. Finally, we oriented ourselves and proceeded on our way.

I heard someone clear his throat. I stopped, laying a hand on Snyder's arm to caution him. Just then, the moon emerged from a bank of heavy clouds and, in its light, I saw our 2nd Battalion chaplain, Reverend Basler, standing quietly under a tree, his head bent in prayer.

But we had a serious mission, so we angled toward him.

I cleared my throat respectfully. "Have you seen Major Miller, Sir?" I asked.

"Why do you want Major Miller, boys?"

"Captain Thompson wants to check one of Major Miller's orders."

"He's asleep over there, under that tree," Chaplain Basler said.

"Asleep?" I said incredulously. "How could he be asleep when he just ordered us to be prepared to attack at once?"

"He never sent any such order. He's been asleep, right there, for three hours. I can vouch for that; I've been standing sentry."

"Then who sent us that message?"

"Probably one of the German spies. They pull such tricks, you know. You boys had better get right back to Captain Thompson and stop him. Have him send warnings to the other company commanders in your sector as well."

We lost no time in thanking him and returning to our posts. When I told the Captain what the chaplain had said, he grinned in quiet satisfaction. "I just knew there was something wrong with that order," he said. "I just felt it in my bones." And he sent messengers to all the other commanders.

As I settled down for the night, I thanked God for the Captain's sound instincts and the chaplain's prayerful sentry duty that had probably prevented a terrible slaughter. With considerable satisfaction, I thought that the Boche spy was probably waiting in some sheltered glade to pick off whatever stupid doughboys had fallen for his scurvy trick. As I drifted peacefully off, I hoped he didn't get a wink of sleep all night.

At dawn's first foggy light, a legitimate order came through for Company F to start over the hill. The first wave sprang out, bayonets fixed, and had begun their torturous advance through the barbed wire when, from every direction, German machine-gun fire assaulted them. Many of them crumbled at once. The second wave—which included me—lay waiting to follow them, horrified by their dying screams. Our platoon commander, seeing the carnage, shouted down the line, "Hit the dirt; don't follow!"

The next few minutes were among the worst of the war for me as we lay, helpless to aid, listening to our friends being torn to pieces by gunfire. No wonder the French considered the Hindenberg line unbreakable!

After what seemed an eternity of horror, the survivors began to make their halting way back, helping the wounded through the murderous barbed wire. Killed were Sergeant Burford and Privates William Brown and Claude Rock of Oklahoma. Lieutenant Connell was wounded.

Huntingdon, too, lost one son, Private Billy Lister. I remembered the day back home when the kid, then only sixteen, had come to enlist. His mother was a cook at Juniata College and had violently opposed his enlisting. Sergeant Flocko Moyer had persuaded her, saying that the draft was imminent. She might as well let the boy go with his own friends—who'd look after him—than with strangers, later, when his draft number came up. So, reluctantly, she'd allowed him to leave with Company F.

Ironically, it fell to Sergeant Moyer to release Billy from the barbed wire in which he'd been trapped and shot and carry him back to the dressing station where the boy died soon after. Flocko had done his best to look after Billy but it just wasn't enough.

Private Harry Humphries, a Scottdale replacement and member of my own squad, had his lower jaw blown away. I helped lift him onto the stretcher that would take him to the dressing station where he died. A few days later, Humphries and the other dead at Le Chene Tondu were buried at the edge of the Argonne Forest. He had a special girl back home who wrote to him often, always enclosing a few sticks of gum in her pink, scented letters. She also sent him homemade fudge and little cakes which he shared with us. We all kidded him about his billet-doux. He would just grin proudly. He liked me and often shared the gum with me. I thought how heartbroken his girl would be to learn her handsome, brave sweetheart was gone. Since it was the duty of squad leaders to open the letters and packages sent to the deceased and return them, writing a note of explanation to the sender, I had the responsibility of opening several of Harry's pink letters. With misty eyes, I skimmed quickly over the tender passages and wrote his sweetheart a note, kind as I could make it, telling her he died a hero's death. I spared her the details. In closing, I wrote, "I am taking the liberty of keeping the gum you enclosed. I hope you understand, Harry would really want me to; he always shared the gum you sent with me. God bless and keep you." I didn't sign my name. I really wouldn't have wanted to ever have to tell her how her handsome boy had been mutilated before he died.

Private Edward Hecker of Cochranton was wounded and later died. Private Charles Jackson of Spring City was killed.

Among the wounded who recovered were Privates Emil Smail of Leechburg, John Hogan, either from Franklin or a replacement from the draft pool. There were some others whose names I failed to record and, I'm afraid, have forgotten. Private Harry Lukehart and Corporal William Hess of Huntingdon each received their second gunshot wounds of the war and Private Earl Pollock of Huntingdon, his first. Men who I saw making repeated trips into the fray to pull wounded comrades to safety and, in my opinion, ought to have gotten commendations for bravery under fire, were Corporal James Bottomfield, Private Puss Hawn of Huntingdon and the fatherly Private First Class Bob Appleby of Mount Union, Sergeant Ross Perrine from Franklin and Sergeant Arthur Gibbs from Cleveland, Ohio, all of whom sustained some wounds in the Argonne. When I think of these brave men, I know the true meaning of the Bible verse: Greater love hath no man than that he would lay down his life for his friends.

Later, when it was all over, we learned that breaking the nigh-invincible Hindenberg line cost the AEF dearly. Over 300,000 shells were poured against the foe. American divisions taking part in the campaign were the 78th, 77th, 28th, 82nd, 35th, 91st, 37th, 79th, 4th, 80th and 33rd. Our own 28th was situated astraddle the Argonne ridge in the very thickest part of the forest. In the impenetrable depths, frequently, foot soldiers outdistanced our 142 Whippet tanks and the 73 heavier French tractor-type ones.

The 2nd Battalion clung doggedly to its position on the hillside. After dark, at last, we could retreat in comparative safety to a railway track in the valley below so that the artillery could blast the Fritzies before we tried to advance again.

This was the enemy's last stand and they were determined to hold it at any cost, not wanting the Allies to sweep through their homeland. They'd been notorious at tearing up other folks' countries, raping and murdering French and Belgium women and children; I suppose they thought *their* loved ones would be subjected to similar insults if we broke across the border. So they threw everything they had against us there in the Argonne.

Overhead, countless Allied aircraft, French, Belgium, British and American, flew together toward Germany. They dropped no bombs on the forest itself; there was far too much danger of killing Allied fighting men.

Eventually we fought our way through to a comparatively quiet place where the boys of Company F were able to get a little badly-needed sleep, disturbed only occasionally by falling shells. At nightfall, we moved to a nearby road and began to angle again. At last, as dark fell, we were ordered to stop and rest as we waited for the kitchens to catch up to us. They did, near midnight, and though the meal they served was pressed beef, which the English called bully meat and the French called monkey meat, bread, doughnuts and coffee, nothing I had ever eaten before or since tasted as good. As soon as we'd eaten, the kitchens departed, taking food to other starving doughboys, and we crawled off the road to sleep again.

During the night, a shell hit a tree under which I and some others were sleeping. While none of us was seriously hurt, the shock turned us icy cold. At daybreak, the attack began in earnest. The 111th were routed from the ridge they'd taken, the same hill where we'd already lost so many men. We, the 112th, were now to advance through the 111th's line and attack the enemy with bayonets and hand grenades.

We got about 50 yards before the slaughter, from machine guns and Minnenwerfers, began, tearing great holes in our lines. Those of us not hit, threw ourselves face down on the ground, which was covered by brightly-colored autumn leaves, made more brilliant yet by the blood of the dead and dying. I heard a scream ahead of me and looked up to see a body being literally rolled over and over like a log by machine-gun fire. It thumped against a tree trunk. I saw that it was an Oil City boy, Private First Class William E. Brown. Private First Class Ray Brown of Oil City was wounded the same day. I don't know if they were related.

Thank God, the regimental commander saw the futility of trying to advance farther and shouted the order to retreat. We did so, literally crawling on our bellies, expecting every second to share the fate of Private First Class Brown. When we reached safety, we were able to count our losses.

A partial list of our casualties in this advance were: Lieutenant Victor Voltz of Franklin; Private Ole Berger, Private Joe Davens, Private First Class Raymond Fish of Centerville, Private Norm Hovis of Franklin, and Private Owen Jones of East Brady; Privates Orthello Miller, Gordon Hardy, and Frank Kurtz (gassed), Corporal Edward Shoff, all of Huntingdon; draftee replacements Privates Singeloni, Lloyd Cummings, Charles Frost of West Manayunk, Dominick Furana of Republic, Louis Kruse, Private First Class Stanley Kapas, and Private John Cooper, who later died of his wounds.

Killed in the engagement were: Corporal Harold Anderson of Franklin, draftee replacements Private Harry Fasbender, Private Charles Jackson of Spring City and Private Marciano Bassetti.

Later, the 111th and 112th combined in a drive against the line and broke through at last, since the Germans, now sustaining extreme pressure on their flank from the Allied forces coming from Verdun, were in full retreat.

We spend several hours caring for our many wounded. We moved about openly, confident that the danger from the retreating enemy was past. Then a swishing shot near my head sent me diving for the forest floor once again. Obviously another of their chained-to-the-tree's gunners was still about. As I waited for someone else in a less vulnerable position to spot him, I heard a voice close at hand.

"Help me; don't leave me here."

I recognized my cousin, Tony Maier's voice. Lifting my head cautiously, I noticed the unmistakeable path of machine-gun fire through the bracken and leaves, but not my cousin.

"Where are you, Tony?" I murmured.

"Behind a tree."

Directly ahead of me stood a big tree, the only one large enough to be concealing him. I took a deep breath, leapt to my feet and ran for its shelter, reaching it just as the concealed gunner started firing again. Tony was stretched out on the ground a little to the right of the tree.

"Don't leave me, Zeb," he pleaded, trying to move toward me.

"I won't. But lie still; you'll only draw his fire," I commanded.

I waited until the line of fire moved off to the left of the tree, then leapt out and pulled him into the tree's shelter. He was white as death and coagulated blood like chunks of liver pooled in the leaves where he'd been lying. I examined him the best I could and saw that the bullet had entered his thigh and taken an upward path; its copper-colored nose was protruding at his hipbone. He'd lost an excessive amount of blood.

Pinned down as we were, we had to wait for a stretcher-bearer to reach him, but, at last, a man carrying a stretcher under his arm came up the hill on the sheltered side of the tree. Between us, we got Tony on the litter and away from immediate danger.

Another stretcher-bearer came forward to relieve me and I asked him if he had a cigarette. He gave one to me and I lighted it and put it between Tony's pale lips.

"Thanks, Zebbie," he said faintly. I knew the thanks was for more than the cigarette.

"It's okay, Tony," I said. I thought of how his dad, my Uncle Christ, and his mother, my mother's older sister, Aunt Jenny, had commanded me to look after Tony when we left home. "You just get well or Aunt Jenny and Uncle Christ will wear me out," I added. I tried to hide my distress at the ghastly way he looked. I never thought he could possibly survive to reach home.

But the son-of-a-gun did. In fact, he beat the rest of us home, for which I thanked God. I shuddered to think of going home to face Aunt Jenny and Uncle Christ without him.

I returned to help with the others. The only original member of my squad left intact after this engagement was Private Melvin Mong of Franklin, who received a battlefield promotion to corporal. By now, the gunner had been taken out but we moved cautiously anyhow.

I found Private Jimmy Bottomfield of Huntingdon bending over one of the draftee replacements whose leg, already nearly severed by a shell blast, had been hit by a falling tree.

The leg was attached to the barely conscious boy only by a few ligaments and shreds of flesh. Even if moving the huge tree had been possible, the leg was beyond saving.

"It's got to come off," Jimmy muttered, more to himself than to me. "We can't lift him out of there until we take it off."

I looked at Jimmy and swallowed. Just then, George Godard and another stretcher-bearer came over the hill toward us, an empty litter between them.

"Ye gods, a gift from heaven," Jimmy said.

He was all brisk business. He pulled off his helmet and set it on the ground like a basin. "Put all your iodine and bandages in there," he commanded.

We complied as Jimmy took a razor blade from his pack and, breaking his own vial of iodine, poured it over the blade.

"Now, two of you hold him down. Though, to tell the truth, I doubt he'll feel it."

The two stretcher-bearers did as he ordered.

I stared down at the kid's pale face. He hardly seemed to know what was happening; I supposed he was in shock. Deftly, Jimmy severed the remaining flesh and ligaments and slapped the iodine-soaked bandages to the stump. They were soon red; we could only hope the iodine would serve to stave off infection. Quickly, we lifted the boy onto the waiting stretcher. Jimmy calmly lit a cigarette and, bending over, thrust it between the boy's lips before George and his partner hauled him away.

For that day's work, Jimmy earned the nickname "Doctor" and so we Company F boys called him that for the rest of his life. When we all returned home, Jimmy married my cousin, Louise, Tony Maier's sister. Once, I asked him if he thought the boy whose leg he'd taken off had lived.

"Oh, yes, he did," Jimmy said.

"How did you find out?" I asked.

"When things calmed down a little, I went to see him at the hospital. I asked him to write me and tell me how he got along," he said. "He's doin' fine."

That boy was only one of many who owed their lives to Jimmy Bottomfield's courage under fire.

Our wounded having been taken care of and the able-bodied among us fed and rested, we finally organized to continue the offensive. Late on the following afternoon, we began the advance westward to a crossroads where, by prearrangement, we were to rendezvous with the 1st and 3rd Battalions.

The next morning, the 2nd Battalion started the attack on the enemy positions with machine guns and grenades. The 1st and 3rd were to leap-frog through our lines. However, the order came to abandon the frontal attack, circle Le Chene Tondu, and proceed up the Aire River valley to Appremont to support the 55th Brigade. This would put us in position to attack Chatel Chehery.

On the night of October 5, Lieutenant Colonel Shannon and other battalion commanders of the 112th formed a patrol and covered the ground to the approaches of Chatel Chehery, which the Germans still held. While thus reconnoitering, this patrol was surrounded by the enemy and couldn't get back to our lines until the morning of the seventh, where the gallant Lieutenant Colonel Shannon died of a wound he'd received the day before. The information the patrol had gleaned was invaluable, deciding the high command to use the 28th and 82nd Divisions in a major thrust to clear the Argonne Forest of the enemy, once and for all, instead of wasting our strength in minor local skirmishes.

Around 3 AM on the morning of October 8, the 112th left the Appremont area to take up positions along the Aire. The 2nd Battalion spearheaded the attack on Chatel Chehery where, with the 1st Battalion, we scaled the cliffs behind which the town lay. Meanwhile, the 3rd Battalion was enduring some of the stiffest resistance of the war, but they, too, managed to hold their position. The deeper we drove the Hun, the more desperate they became. By evening, we—the 2nd Battalion—had pushed the enemy 2 kilos west, twice as far as any other division involved. There we held them until relieved by the 82nd Division on the night of the ninth.

Private Harold Helsel was wounded for the second time, this time severely enough to be sent home, but, all in all, casualties were remarkably light.

Exhausted, hungry, worn out with the sights we'd seen, we marched back to Montblainville, proud of the job we'd done. Later, when we read the general orders, we learned just how justified was our pride. The high commands of France, Great Britain, and America had all extolled the bravery of all units of the 28th Division during the Argonne campaign.

Company F had, truly, helped administer the coup de grace to the Boche.

CHAPTER 10

On Leave

At Montblainville, rumors flew: We were heading for a rest camp; the Allies had pushed the offensive clear to Germany; the Kaiser had surrendered; and, we were heading home.

All too soon we learned they were only rumors.

Lieutenant Colonel Shannon was killed October 7, 1918, so Captain John Graff was given command of the 112th. Orders came to march to Neuvily. The everlasting rain had finally let up and, though we'd thought France would never dry out, the well-drained dirt road we marched on soon had us all choking in a huge cloud of dust.

"I've spit out enough 'dobe bricks to build me a fair-sized house," complained one border veteran as we trudged along.

On to Aubreville, where there was a railhead, to Provis, where trucks carried us to Commercy and other towns along the Woevre front. Company F landed in a town called Gironville. None of them were rest camps.

So persistent were the rumors that, at last, Colonel Rickards was compelled to issue a bulletin to the troops, which read: "While the news of the past few days has been gratifying, it does not terminate the war and we must not permit it to turn our attention from further perfecting our organization for the tasks set for the AEF, to bring the Hun and his colleagues to unconditional surrender . . . ."

The day after his message to the troops, the brief spell of clear weather was over and we were on the march again in a cold, persistent rain. Our destination was the Thiaucourt-Pannes sector. Despite the rain, we could see a German observation balloon in the sky ahead with dark puffs of smoke from antiaircraft guns billowing around it.

We relieved the French and American troops, including the 147th Regiment of the Ohio National Guard, which had been holding the Woevre front for some time. The sector was fairly quiet; the two forces facing each other were making no major efforts against each other at the time. Regimental

Headquarters had been established at a town called Beney, the machine-gun company at St. Benoit, and headquarter and supply companies at Pannes.

The 1st Battalion was assigned the right sector of the woods surrounding Dampvitoux, Companies E and F relieved the front-line troops, G and H—now composed mostly of draftees—became Brigade Reserve, and the 3rd Battalion took the left sector.

The 28th Division, because of its outstanding performance in breaking the Hindenberg line and driving the enemy from the Argonne Forest, had been chosen to spearhead the attack on Metz. Having lost so many men in the Argonne, Company F had to be brought up to battle strength from reserve units. The influenza pandemic that was sweeping America— it took the lives of Private Bill Edwards' wife and infant son—had taken its toll on the army as well.

In any case, when Company F went into the front line at Thiaucourt, there weren't too many familiar faces in the ranks. It was a particularly dismal place. For a wonder, there were no trenches, dugouts or shelters from enemy fire except for shallow ditches in the hillside under the endlessly dripping trees. The mere slit in the ground I drew, at least had the amenity of a sodden blanket as carpeting. Otherwise, I'd have been wallowing in mud like a pig in a sty. As it was, there was nothing to do but read our clothing for cooties, remove our sodden shoes and socks in a vain attempt to let our diseased feet heal, and—when the occasion allowed— visit with each other.

F company mechanic, Horace Corbin, had dropped in to my burrow for such a visit one evening after bringing the food wagon to our position when a German plane began dropping propaganda leaflets on our lines. They were written in English, using doughboy slang. While they were intended to get *us* to surrender, they merely furnished us with some welcome entertainment as we lay in our muddy holes. Certainly, old Horace and I, sitting there with our ruined feet aloft, laughed fit to bust at them. I kept some of them, reproduced below.

THE GERMAN PEOPLE OFFER PEACE

The will of the people is the highest law. The German people want quickly to end this slaughter. The new German popular government therefore has offered an ARMISTICE and has declared itself ready for "Peace" on the basis of justice and reconciliation of the nations.

It is the will of the German people that it should live and let live in peace with all peoples honestly and loyally.

What has this new German Popular Government done so far to put into practice the will of the people and to prove its good and upright intentions?

(a) The New German Government has appealed to President Wilson to bring about the peace.

IT HAS RECOGNIZED AND ACCEPTED ALL THE PRINCIPLES WHICH PRESIDENT WILSON PROCLAIMED AS A BASIS FOR A GENERAL LASTING PEACE AMONG NATIONS.

(b) The New German Government has solemnly declared its readiness to evacuate Belgium and restore it.

(c) The New German Government is ready to come to an honest understanding with France about ALSACE-LORRAINE.

(d) The New German Government has restricted the U-boat war. No passenger steamers not carrying troops or war materials will be attacked in future.

(e) The New German Government has declared that it will withdraw all German troops back over the German frontier.

(f) The New German Government has asked the Allied governments to name commissions to agree upon the practical measure of evacuating Belgium and France.

These are the deeds of the New Popular Government. Can these be called mere words, bluff or propaganda?

Who is to blame if an Armistice is not called now? Who is to blame if daily thousands of brave soldiers needlessly have to shed their life blood and die?

Who is to blame if hitherto undestroyed towns and villages of France and Belgium sink in ashes?

Who is to blame if hundreds and thousands of unhappy women and children are driven from their homes to hunger and freeze?

The German People offers its hand in peace.

The following one was really a doozy:

ATTENTION BRAVE AMERICAN SOLDIERS

Why are you in this war? Stop and think a minute! What are you fighting for? You want to see your father, mother, wives and children, don't you? And you want to return to the United States again. Why don't you do so? It's easy! Just step over the lines and live in comfort at the expense of the German government till the war is over and we will send you safely home. Isn't that a lot better than to rot in the shell holes of France?

We have no quarrel with the soldier boys in their faded gray on the other side of No-Man's land. What do you need to care who wins the war? You had a lot better be home fighting the Trusts in your own country.

Think it over and then step across the line and join the many other Americans living in luxury behind the German lines.

Act quick! Join us while the going's good.

Obviously, the German propaganda machine, meant to weaken our morale, was destroying theirs. However, the German lines were so close to ours that we could hear—but not understand—their conversations as, no doubt, they heard ours. So, inevitably, one of the suffering German soldiers, our next door neighbors in the Thiacourt sector, knew enough English to translate the poisonous lies. We could almost hear the shattering of their illusions as they realized they'd been had. They began crawling out of their holes in droves, hands on heads, jabbering "Kamerad" or, in halting English, "Germany is kaput; we don't want to die for lost cause."

Indeed, it seemed to us that Germany was kaput. It would only be a matter of time.

However, we still dispatched patrols at night, though we never fired a shot. The only enemies we hadn't defeated were the infernal cooties, our own wet clothes and the bitter nights.

Once, when the 2nd Battalion was relieved from front-line duty, we were able to obtain baths in an old German bathhouse. The respite from torment was brief since we had no clean garments to don and had to crawl back into our filthy ones, still teeming with cooties.

However, as October wore on in sodden misery, all indications were that an armistice would soon be signed. Anticipation might well have died without the constant struggle just to endure as we waited. We spent hours reading our clothing and burning the little beasts, or slogging through knee-deep mud in the perpetual cold rain. Winter was rapidly approaching and the entire 112th was billeted in unheated barns and chicken coops. Finding enough food was a constant problem and F company's mess sergeant, Frank Dillon, scrounged far and wide, buying what food he could from the Mess Fund savings.

Those with a franc or two, spent the evenings in the estaminets, nursing a glass of beer or a spoonful of cognac. The little taverns were warmer and drier than our billets and the barmaids were marginally congenial, at least as long as our money held out. To be sure, the girls labored under the illusion that all doughboys were millionaires and seemed to think us mighty cheap for thinking the price of one drink was enough for a few hours of respite from our farm sheds. So, though we sympathized with the much longer period of warfare the French had endured, we doughboys, naturally, resented their lack of gratitude for our help in whipping the Kaiser.

I was sitting in my usual post, a wet trench, trying to ignore the ice-cold torrent that was pouring around me, the day a runner came from headquarters with a message for me.

"Corporal Baker, you're going on leave," he said.

I won't repeat the tongue-lashing I gave him, ending with my considered opinion of the character of any doughboy who'd tell another soldier he was going on leave as a joke.

"I'm not joking, Corporal," he said indignantly. "What kinda' heel you think I am? And I ain't so fond o' this damned rain I'd come all the way out here just to get off a joke. Now get back to headquarters!"

In a daze, I crawled out of the muddy trench and followed the runner back to Pannes. Apparently the War Department, recognizing the discontent of homesick doughboys as we waited for the powers-that-be to hammer out the terms of an armistice, had instituted a series of leaves to French watering places and pleasure resorts.

When we arrived at headquarters, two of my Company F buddies, Fred Flake and Jimmy "Foxy" Lewis, and a Sergeant Art Gibbs of Cleveland, Ohio were sitting on a bench wearing expressions like penniless kids staring through a candy store window.

"Zeb, they say twelve of us are goin' on leave," Fred said, incredulously.

"To some fancy spa!" Foxy added.

"I wonder if they've got cooties there?" Fred asked.

"They will after they let us in," Foxy countered.

"They won't *let* us in until we get rid of our pets," Fred said scornfully. "And it wouldn't hurt if you dumped your chaw, either, Foxy."

"You're right," Foxy said, self-consciously looking around for a suitable dumping ground.

The truck that was to take us arrived then and we climbed eagerly aboard amidst the cheers of doughboys from other units already aboard. We squeezed in beside them and the truck took off, over dark and rutted forest roads, unloading us at a railhead. Here, we boarded forty-and-eight boxcars. When the train was jammed full of exuberant doughboys, we departed for Nancy.

We arrived the next morning, cold, wet and nearly starved. Red Cross representatives met us and led us to the public bathhouse connected to a big hotel. They gave us huge bars of soap, not the little, bitty one-inch blocks we'd been issued in our packs. And, when they told us to put *all* our clothing in a rubbish can, we really thought we'd died and gone straight to heaven.

We wallowed in those hot, soapy baths as only weary, dirty soldiers could, emerging only when we could no longer suppress our guilt over ignoring the cries of other doughboys waiting *their* turn in the baths.

The Red Cross even provided us with razors and new *clean* clothing. As we looked in the mirrors at ourselves, though we were decidedly leaner and more care-worn than when we left the crossing boats at Calais, we thought we weren't half-bad.

Our guardian angels of the Red Cross then ushered us into a big club room full of easy chairs and NEWSPAPERS and BOOKS! To those of us who were avid readers, this was heaven. A heaven deferred, however, by a call to an even more immediate need, FOOD.

We were summoned to a big dining-room that had been set aside for our use where waiters were preparing to serve us a meal fit for a king. When we'd finished eating it, almost licking the plates, one of the angels masquerading as a sergeant, smiled and said, "How would you boys like to go to Aix-les-Bains in the French Alps?"

We nearly deafened him with our enthusiastic acceptance of the offer. Personally, I thought we'd blundered into an Arabian Nights' fairy tale.

We marched back to the railway. Only, this time, we boarded first-class railway cars like the respectable soldier citizens we were, though Fred—his eye gleaming with fun—kept muttering about missing his cooties. We told him to shut up.

We rode all that night and part of the next day, finally arriving at the beautiful spa, high in the mountains.

Everywhere we looked in this paradise of towering mountains, luxury hotels and gambling casinos, were well-dressed, pleasant-faced, friendly people. We were assigned rooms and even advanced some money, first signing slips permitting the army to take it from our future pay. Then we were escorted to a big, marble-fronted hospital on a street named for John Pierpont Morgan, the American millionaire who'd given the hospital to the French people. Here, we were to be examined by a physician, after which, for seven days, we were on our own.

Seven days, with money in our pockets, to play like children in this heaven on earth!

But, first, we had to endure physicals. When it came my turn, the doctor, an army major, stuck a thermometer into my mouth and reached for my wrist to take my pulse.

"How do you feel, soldier?" he asked.

Talking with difficulty around the thermometer, I said, "Just fine, Sir."

"Dysentery?"

"Sure, everybody has a little dysentery."

He frowned and kept his finger on my pulse. He pulled the thermometer from my mouth and stared at it, frowning more than ever. He gave me a stern look.

"103 degrees. So, you feel fine, do you?" he said in a chiding voice.

"Sure I do, Sir."

"Well, you're *not* fine. Go to your hotel room, gather your belongings, and report back here, immediately. That's an order." He stared at me sternly. "And, if you take it into your head to ignore it, I'll send an MP to find you."

I stifled my groans. I couldn't disobey. I looked around for Foxy or Fred but they'd already passed through the line and were nowhere in sight. There was nothing to do but go back to my room and get my gear.

Foxy, who'd been assigned to share my room, was lying on his bed, a bottle of whiskey, about two-thirds full, beside him. "Been waitin' for you. Hurry up, Zeb, let's hit the town!"

"I can't, Foxy. The doctor ordered me back to the hospital."

"How come?"

"Says I'm too sick to go on leave."

"Hell, I'm as sick as you and my doc said I was fine. You're just having fun with me, ain't you, Zeb?"

"No, it's true."

"You mean, you came all the way across France to the best resort in the whole damned country, got rid o' your lice, and now they're gonna put you in the damned *hospital*?" Suddenly, he began to laugh.

I stared at him speculatively. "Tell you what. Why don't you dump that bottle of whiskey down the commode and come on over to the hospital with me. Like you said, you're as sick as I am—"

He stared at me with the contempt my suggestion deserved.

"I ain't so sick I'd deliberately check into the hospital when I got a whole week in Aux-les-Bains! I *smell* good now; the little mademoiselles will be nicer to me. As for being sick, I'll just take some good, long belts on my bottle and sleep until noon tomorrow and I'll be good as new."

"The hell you will. You'll land in jail without me to take care of you." I sighed deeply and picked up my writing materials. "That's okay, Jimmy, I'm glad you're getting to go," I said, and stalked out of the room. I loved that man like my brother and I *was* glad he was getting leave in this classy resort, but, I must admit, at that moment, I was so jealous of him I could cheerfully have wrung his neck if it would have gotten *me* seven days' leave.

My steps dragged as I walked back to the hospital, thinking I was the most unfortunate damned doughboy in the whole AEF. The doctor was waiting to admit me. Shortly, they'd divested me of my unlousy clothes and ordered me into bed. At least I'd be able to catch up on my diary keeping. And sleep in a real, *clean* bed. I had just reached for my pen and notebook when a brisk, elderly nurse came in with a big glass of castor oil.

"Drink it all down, soldier," she said and stood there to see that I did. As I swallowed the noxious stuff, I thought bitterly of Jimmy's bottle of whiskey.

With a nod of satisfaction, she took the empty glass from me and turned toward the door. "Your supper will be here soon," she said as she left the room. At least they intended to feed me. I waited impatiently for the promised supper. She'd said it would be arriving soon.

It did, the whole glass of orange juice and a thin slice of dry toast. I tried my best to imagine it was a big, juicy beefsteak with mashed potatoes which was probably what Fred and Foxy were eating about now.

To make a long, unpleasant story short, they kept me there in that damned John Pierpont Morgan hospital, purging and starving and sleeping until the day before we were to report back to Pannes, when, taking pity on me, they finally ordered my release. I hurried over to the hotel to find Foxy lying on his bed, still a few swallows left in his bottle, and looking a whole lot worse than I did.

"I been sick the whole damned leave," he complained.

"You should have come into the hospital with me," I said.

"I wish I had."

"Oh, you should have. They served us steak and potatoes and chocolate cake most nights," I lied. "And my nurse! Oo la la!"

"Oh, that sounds wonderful. I was too sick to go out most o' the time."

"Well, come on out with me now; I want to see the town."

"I already seen the damned town," he grumbled, but he did pull himself off the bed and accompanied me. We hadn't gone very far until he had to use one of the comfort stations along the street which the practical French had in abundance in every city.

We ate a good dinner in the hotel . . . at least *I* did. We paid the bill and started down the street. I saw another establishment that sold ice-cream.

"Come on, Foxy, I gotta have some of that," I said.

"You just ate enough to keep the company goin' for a day, includin' ice cream for dessert," he complained.

"I know, that's what whetted my appetite for ice cream."

He came in and watched me demolish three helpings. When the proprietor asked him if he cared for any, he just shook his head and groaned.

We walked down the pleasant street, gazing in the shop windows, admiring the rugged Cat's Tooth Peak on Mount Renard. We took a cab to Lake Bourget and walked around, admiring the sights. There were glass-bottomed boats that took passengers on a tour of the lake but, glancing at Foxy's green face, I decided not to suggest it.

When we passed a photographer's studio, though, I said, "Come on, Jimmy, let's get our pictures taken."

"I don't need to do that; I know what I look like," he groused.

"Send one to your mother."

"*She* knows what I look like, too."

"Hell, Foxy, when we get home, even *you* might get a girl friend who'll want your picture."

"When I'm back home, *she'll* know what I look like, too," he said reasonably.

So I alone had my picture taken. I found the post office and sent copies home. Then, since Jimmy was really sick and we had to start back to camp first thing the next morning, we returned to the hotel.

We returned the same way we'd come, first-class carriages to Commercy, forty-and-eight cars to the railhead, and trucks to Pannes. Naturally, considering the second and third stages of our journey back, by the time we reached camp, we were all repopulated with our little friends. And, somewhere on the way, a painful swelling of my neck and throat began to distract me. When we stumbled from the trucks at Pannes, I could no longer swallow. I lined up for the first sick call in Pannes.

The doctor took one look at me, touched my swollen neck and said, "Soldier, you've got the mumps."

He ordered me to sit down with the other soldiers awaiting an ambulance to carry them to Tours. I sat there, sunk in gloom.

By now, Fred and Foxy had returned to our unit and, when some of my buddies heard what had happened to me, they came to see me before the ambulance arrived. They kidded me and told me if I didn't hurry and get well, I'd miss marching out with the company for an attack on Metz which was rumored to be imminent. I had to fight back the tears; since the beginning, never once had I failed to march into battle with Company F.

On November 10, in the mumps ward of the hospital, I heard that long-range guns were shelling the border city of Metz. When the artillery had done its preliminary work, the 112th would go over the top without me.

But at 11 AM on November 11, the armistice was signed; it was over. Thank God, it was over.

The patients cheered as loudly as their swollen faces would allow. What an ignominious way to celebrate the end of the war! How I longed to clasp the hands of the men I'd marched with, suffered with, fought with all these months. But never mind, it was over.

All over the hospital, strained voices asked one question: "When will we be going home?"

Home. Dear God, home! We'd survived a war that had killed nine million people and we were going home.

But no one yet knew when.

CHAPTER 11

Armistice

I remained in the hospital until the following day, when, with a number of other newly-released patients, I marched to what was euphemistically called a casual camp on the outskirts of Pannes. It resembled Rest Camp 6 at Calais, except that, instead of black sand, the whole place was a sea of mud. The war might be over; the mud we had always with us.

On the morning of November 14, a call went through the camp for any men from the 112th to report to a sergeant who was to guide me and Private Harold Dorworth of Franklin back to our outfit. Along the way, we picked up Private Orthello Miller of Huntingdon who'd been wounded on October 6. Somewhere, he'd gotten hold of some loaf sugar and a box of chocolates. He shared them with us as we walked.

But, when we reached Pannes, the 112th had already moved out.

"What should we do?" Orthello asked our guide.

The sergeant scratched his head. "Damned if I know."

No one else seemed to know, either.

"How the hell do you lose a whole regiment?" I fumed.

Orthello just smiled. "Take it easy, Zeb. Last I heard, the 112th was headed to Chaumont. We'll catch up."

The sergeant, having discharged his orders, however unsatisfactorily, gave us a disinterested wave and returned to the camp. Miller and Dorworth and I looked at each other for a minute and then started hoofing toward Chaumont.

At Bussieres, we found Headquarters Company living in comparative comfort. When we asked if anyone knew where Company F had landed, a private told us they were camped at a place called Muddy Hollow, just ahead.

The name sounded ominous. We set off again, wondering aloud how a fellow went about being transferred to Headquarters Company where the living was easy. That was only doughboy griping, though. We couldn't wait to see our own comrades, who, when we arrived, greeted us like brothers.

While I'd been away, Company F had lost two more replacement boys, just before the armistice. Major Miller, who had been previously wounded, had been promoted to battalion commander.

We were billeted in a former German camp, situated at the head of a narrow valley. The November bleak hills rose sharply on either side of our bivouac area. The mess hall was only a ramshackle shed, so most of our meals had to be eaten outdoors on tables constructed from sawhorses and planks, while rain or snow pelted us. Our "barracks" consisted of a number of falling-down sheds, each containing tier-on-tier of rough bunks having chicken wire springs and many generations of German and Allied lice. The sheds were so crowded that, when Dorworth and Orthello and I arrived, in order to find anything resembling a sleeping place, we had to crawl in under the lowest bunks, the aisles between being entirely too muddy to spread our bedrolls. The spot I took was right beneath Sergeant Frank "Dixie" Myers of Alexandria.

I can't even begin to describe the misery of those wretched unheated sheds, crawling with vermin, nor of their homesick, demoralized inhabitants who had nothing to do but conjecture why the hell we weren't on our way home. Someone scrounged up a one-burner kerosene stove on which we cooked lumpy oatmeal and condensed milk in our mess kits. In the evenings, there was nothing to do but to play cards and complain.

As I lay on the floor one night, cursing the viciously biting lice, my eyes lit on the kerosene can in the dim moonlight shining through the cracks in the shed walls. Slowly, an idea began forming. The more I thought about it, the more brilliant it seemed. I can only plead temporary insanity induced by hunger, boredom, bitter cold—who the hell ever said hell was *hot*—and my recent illness. I crawled out from under the tier of bunks and removed every stitch of my lice-ridden clothing, turning a deep shade of blue in the process. Dousing my handkerchief with kerosene, I applied the stuff liberally to the inside of all my clothing. Let the damned lice feast on *that* for awhile. Grinning with satisfaction, I donned my clothes again and, in a glow of warm contentment, crawled back under Dixie's bunk.

All of a sudden, my skin felt as if I'd fallen into a vat of lye. With a howl that woke every man in the building, I scooted out from under the bunks and began frantically disrobing until I was as naked as the day I was born.

Dixie reared up, rubbing his eyes. "What the devil's the matter with you, Zeb?" he demanded.

But I had thrown the door wide open and was already on my way out to roll in the snow, while everyone in the room added indignant comments: "Who's that, makin' such a fuss?" "Where the hell were you raised, Baker, in an elephant's arse?" "What the hell you been drinkin', Zebbie?"

At last, nearly frozen stiff, I returned to the shed, slammed the door shut, and scrambled into my overcoat, the only garment I'd not doused with kerosene.

"You gonna sleep in that, Zebbie?" Dixie asked.

"Yes," I snapped and crawled back under his bunk where I spent the rest of the night with a sore hide but with considerably fewer lice. The next day, squatting in the snow in my overcoat, I washed my clothes—inadequately enough—in the only pail we had.

These interminable days of suffering dragged on and on as the Allied Powers hammered out the terms of peace. Already, Kaiser Wilhelm II had been given asylum in the Netherlands. It seemed to me he got off remarkably easy for all the suffering he'd caused.

To my surpise, the army selected me to go to southern France to a brigade school for training in chemical warfare.

"I don't know why they want me to learn more about *war*," I groused. "I want to go home."

"Well, we aren't likely to be going home until spring," Bob Appleby said reasonably. "In the meantime, you might as well enjoy spending Christmas away from Muddy Hollow."

I certainly agreed, of course, but, as I made my way to Bussieres, I couldn't help thinking how lost I'd felt when I'd been discharged from the hospital, only to find my friends gone.

In Bussieres, I joined up with some fellows from the 110th Infantry, and Private Fred Endres from another company of the 112th, who was going to musketry school. The club room where we assembled was actually *heated*, which made me quickly doze off in my chair. Shortly, I was awakened from a vivid dream of being back on the ridge at Le Chene Tondu by someone calling my name.

"Corporal Baker. Are you Corporal Baker?"

I opened my eyes to see a belligerent-looking sergeant leaning over me.

I scrambled to my feet. "Yes, Sergeant, I'm Corporal Baker."

"This ain't no slumber party, you know," he said sourly. "Shake a leg." Then, turning to the others, he shouted, "All right, you yard birds, outside and fall in."

We picked up our gear and followed him outside, exchanging worried glances. It sure looked like we'd drawn one of those petty, power-wielding non-coms (non-commissioned officers) whose chief purpose in life is making their subordinates miserable.

We boarded a railway car, the sergeant holding all our tickets. The train had to stop frequently for fuel at which time the sergeant ordered us all off the train while he and two of his flunkies also refueled at a nearby estaminet. Since the sergeant held the tickets, the train couldn't continue until he was back aboard so Fred and I and a couple of the 110th fellows had one drink a piece, which we each nursed.

The sergeant, who'd had several, began badgering three young poilus sitting at a nearby table.

"We come over here and won the damned war for you," he crowed. "Least you could do is admit we're better fightin' men than you."

The poilus just smiled politely. The old woman proprietor of the estaminet looked on worriedly.

Suddenly, the sergeant plucked the uniform cap off the head of the smallest poilu and, casting it contemptuously aside, jammed his own hat down on the little Frenchman's head. The kid, as if determined not to rile the crude sergeant, still smiled politely.

The sergeant picked up the wine bottle from their table and nearly drained it, not stopping until only a finger of the wine remained. He swaggered over to a table where an old man sat eating a meagre meal of cheese and bread and upended the bottle on him.

That did it. The three French soldiers moved as one man. They picked up the sergeant and headed toward the door. My new friends and I gladly moved out of the way to give them room as they dumped the sergeant unceremoniously on his ass in the street.

His two companions made a beeline back to the waiting train, leaving their drinking buddy alone on the cobbles. The poilus quietly returned to the estaminet.

The sergeant, catching sight of Fred and me and the other two doughboys, jumped to his feet. "Did you see what them damned frogs just did to me?" he roared. "Let's go back in there and teach them a lesson."

"Nuts to you, mister," Fred said, "you got exactly what was coming to you."

We turned our backs on him and climbed back aboard the train. I must say, the rest of our journey was completed somewhat more quietly.

The school lasted for two weeks. Unfortunately, the bullying sergeant was in charge of our tickets back north, too. Again, we had to endure his drinking at every stop. At the last fuel stop before rejoining our units, one of the 110th boys protested vigorously.

"We're almost there, Sarge, and the conductor said it would be a short stop. You'll make us miss the train."

"So what? We'll just catch the next one."

"The hell we will! You're not gonna be happy till you've landed us all in the Bastille."

The sergeant thrust out his jaw. "I'm the officer here."

"Yeah, you're the officer, all right, Sergeant Jackass. I got a hundred francs here says you got those stripes after the armistice."

The look on the sergeant's face betrayed the accuracy of that assessment. He slumped down in his seat as the train jerked into motion and we heard little else from him for the rest of the journey.

At Bussieres, Fred and I were concerned by the fact that we saw no 112th boys about. We headed for Muddy Hollow but Company F had gone, leaving it more desolate than ever. We searched the other billeting areas; Fred's unit had also disappeared.

"What a hell of a way to run an army," I muttered. "Now what do we do?"

"Go back to Bussieres," Fred suggested. "Maybe someone there will know what happened to them."

We turned back the way we'd come, plowing through six inches or so of mud the whole way. The proprietor of the boulangerie in town, where the doughboys were wont to buy cold meats when they had the funds, knew only that the entire 112th had left on January 6. He didn't know their destination.

"Maybe they started home without us," Fred said, his expression as doleful as an army mule's.

"They wouldn't do a thing like that . . . would they?" I asked, feeling my own chin moving considerably south.

"Why didn't they leave word of their destination somewhere, so we could follow them?"

"Maybe they wired us at the school and it didn't catch us in time."

"That's probably it. They'd surely have left word *somewhere* if they'd expected us back here."

"Well, what d'you suppose we ought to do?"

"Start lookin' for them," he said.

So we started an odyssey that took us all over France, even to General Pershing's headquarters at Chaumont. Once, at Traveron, we almost caught up with them. They'd been there, but no one knew where they'd gone.

At first, we considered just approaching an MP and explaining how we'd come to be separated from our unit and asking for help. But, the whole country was in an uproar after the armistice and we were honestly afraid of having some overworked MP tell us our reason for being absent from our unit was "a likely story" and throw us into jail as AWOLs.

Civilians and allied soldiers jammed the streets and roads of France, hunting lost relatives, trying to scrounge enough to fend off starvation. Miles of roads and rail lines lay in ruins; the Spanish flu was sweeping the world, on the very heels of the ravenous dogs of war.

We traveled shanks mare for awhile. Then one day, too tired to keep going, we boarded a train and, when the conductor asked for our tickets, we spread our arms in an eloquent pantomime of having none. The conductor good-naturedly let us stay. After that, we tried it often. The French were so grateful for our help in the war that, sometimes, it worked. Often, however, we'd find ourselves unceremoniously escorted from the train at the next stop.

Getting food was not as big a problem. When we'd see an army unit lined up for chow, we'd simply join the line and thrust out our mess kits.

But we—two khaki-clad bums—were always afraid of being arrested as deserters.

Finally, a full two months after finishing brigade school, Fred saw a truck driver near St.-Mihiel with the familiar "bucket of blood" emblem on his arm. He let out a wild whoop and ran toward the truck, his arms waving wildly. I sprinted to keep up.

"You're the prettiest sight we've seen in two months," he said, laughing. "Can you give us a ride?"

The driver grinned broadly and told us to jump aboard.

"Where's the 112th Infantry?" I asked.

"Headquarters Company is at Colombes Les Belles. Pagny La Blanche Cote has some, too."

"Company F?"

"I don't know about F. But they'll know at Colombes Les Belles."

"How far?"

"Just a few miles. I'll drop you off as close as I can and give you directions."

He was as good as his word. In no time at all, we'd each rejoined our own company. The boys of Company F welcomed me back as if I'd been the Prodigal Son and soon filled me in on their adventures. They'd left Bussieres on January 6 and, after an arduous march in the mud, reached Pagny on the tenth. They were soon back to drilling every day.

"Only difference from war is, when we charged a hill before the armistice, there was an enemy waitin' on the other side," Puss said.

"There's as many lice in peacetime as there is in war, Zebbie," Fred Flake declared.

The whole company had one question: when were we going home?

We visited Domremy, the birthplace of Joan of Arc, whose shrine had become a sort of mecca for war-weary doughboys. Indeed, the humble wooden building alleged to have been her birthplace was enclosed with iron railings that didn't keep the soldiers from breaking off chunks as souvenirs, right under the noses of the caretakers. Nearby, a beautiful church in her honor was under construction. We also visited Voucouleurs, where Joan had raised an army to march against England, under the infant king, Henry VI.

At this time, I was promoted to sergeant and given a chevron to sew on my jacket. But a counterorder, rescinding all promotions came from headquarters before I could do so. Our Captain ruefully explained why the promotions were withdrawn. So many draftees had poured into France during the last days of the war that the quota of non-commissioned officers was more than filled. Needless to say, this was a bitter disappointment to us front-line veterans, but, as the French say, c'est le guerre.

The tail end of winter in Pagny was about as exciting as a little girl's piano recital. The boredom was alleviated by Red Gray's brawling when he was drinking. Which was most of the time. Back in Texas, only Lieutenant Corbin and I had been able to do anything with Red when he had a snootful.

Since the Lieutenant had been mustered out at Camp Hancock, controlling Red was up to me. I wondered how he'd managed to stay out of jail while Fred and I had been bumming around France, trying to find the 112th.

One winter night, Sergeant Harry Davis staged a production of *Uncle Tom's Cabin*. Davis, who was tall and cadaverous-looking, played Simon Legree to Baldy Rittenhouse's Uncle Tom and little, blond Whitey Leeper's Little Eva. Cast and audience alike were somewhat the worse for the liquid refreshments consumed. Private Homer Heck staggered to his feet and yelled, "Don't I get a part in this play?"

Davis picked up a lighted candle and thrust it into Homer's hand. "Yeah, you're the footlight. Now sit down before you fall down."

Harriet Beecher Stowe has probably still not stopped spinning. But the production took a bunch of doughboys' minds off their homesickness for an evening.

There was precious little chance of l'amour in Pagny since the only available female was a barmaid in her father's estaminet. She hadn't been young for a very long time. But the inevitable law of supply and demand prevailed and she had a number of doughboys vying for her favors. A sergeant from another company won. He usually stayed at the estaminet until closing when, presumably, he'd bed down with the barmaid. The next day, he'd show up at breakfast, his face covered with scratches.

There were various schools of thought about this little romance: either the mademoiselle spent the night defending her honor, the sergeant liked rough lovemaking, or the lady felt she ought to pretend to fight him off.

We had enough to eat but that's the very best to be said about the food. A member of the regimental band contracted spinal meningitis and died. The rest of the band were promptly quarantined but, fortunately, no one else got it.

A big review of the troops before General Pershing, General Robert Bullard, and some French officers was ordered. We surmised this meant we'd soon be heading home, but the days dragged on and the order didn't come.

By now, most of us were pretty well broke. I parted with the last of the Lugers I'd picked up on the battlefield. I still had a pair of binoculars which I later gave to the girl who became my wife, the wallet with Albert Eggers' papers and photos, a French pocket watch and a German one, and a handful of knives. When I got home, I gave the knives to my brothers. The watches I took to be cleaned and repaired but they mysteriously disappeared from the shop where I'd taken them. So much for the spoils of war.

We were ordered to rebuild the ruined French road and railroad systems. Up until this time, we'd mostly considered the French people our friends. After weeks of working on their damned roads, most of us considered them ingrates at best, crooks at worst. Part of the peace terms were that we help repair the roads destroyed in the war. We thought we'd done enough to drive the Boche back and help end the war.

The 112th organized a theatrical troupe which, during the waning days of that winter, entertained troops all over France. Some of the men from Headquarters Company were John Surra and Granville Lane. Another member was Nathan Cohen, a Company F boy from Philadelphia who'd been a concert violinist for the Philadelphia Philharmonic before entering the service. When the AEF at last returned home, this fine unit remained together, touring the United States for awhile.

At last, in the spring of 1919, we marched to Maxey where trains were waiting to take us on the first leg of our journey home. We sang every step of the way: "Mademoiselle from Armentiers," "The Old Gray Mare," and "Over There." No one attempted the tender "Till We Meet Again" or "My Buddy." Memories of those we loved at home or the good friends we'd left beneath the mud of France would have unmanned us in seconds.

We boarded boxcars at Maxey for the next leg. All along the way, Red Cross and YMCA volunteers gave us good things to eat. We finally reached the Le Mans Forwarding Camp.

The place was a sea of mud which even infiltrated our blankets. Here, we went through the delousing mills, sitting naked in steam-filled rooms while our uniforms were also steamed to kill the vermin. Being free of the cursed little varmints was more than compensation for standing in line in knee-deep mud for food and having no where to eat it when we got it except sitting on our muddy bunks. Unfortunately, this less-than-thorough treatment of the lice only slowed them down for awhile; we weren't really to be shed of them until we were mustered out at Fort Dix.

We were allowed passes into the city and merchants did a brisk business in souvenirs, such as pillows with mottoes like "For my Sweetheart" and "For you, Mother" being the best sellers.

Inevitably, as we waited for orders to sail, some of us got into trouble. Sergeant Harry Davis bailed Fred Flake out of jail for being drunk and disorderly. Even I, unofficial mother hen of the company, imbibed more than usual and took on a couple of Algerian soldiers at a carnival one night. They promptly threw me into the mud. Private First Class Roy Crownover picked me up and hauled me back to camp. Roy lies now beside his brothers, Charlie and Oscar, who'd both been with us on the border, in a little country churchyard. May God rest his faithful soul.

From Le Mans, we rode boxcars to St. Nazaire where, as usual, we were stopped for a time on a siding. We spotted a huge cask marked "VIN", resting on a flatcar on another track and began animatedly discussing how thirsty we all were. One of the thirsty doughboys could stand it no longer; he pulled his revolver and shot a hole in the cask near the top, sending forth a graceful arc of red wine.

A veritable stampede ensued. Doughboys holding out the tin cups each mess kit contained gathered under the red torrent. They were too eager; the closer they got, the greater the force of the wine. Cups went a-flying. As our train lurched, wine-spattered doughboys, some lucky enough to have gotten a portion of the wine, scrambled back aboard. I'm sure Uncle Sam got a sizeable bill for the damage. In this case at least, the bill was justified.

We finally reached St. Nazaire in mid-April where we underwent more physicals, more delousing and getting our records straightened out. The 28th Division was assigned to two ships, taken from Germany as part of the peace agreement. I was to sail on one formerly called *Vaderland*, re-christened *Pocahontas*. The other was called *Olympic*. They bore no resemblance to the beautiful *Aquitania* that had brought us from America. We wouldn't have cared if the *Pocahontas* had been a canoe! We'd been gone a whole year.

Only a year? It seemed like a lifetime. We marched aboard the dirty, crowded ships with thankful hearts that beat in time: home, home, home, home, thank God, we were going home!

The man who made up the passenger list for the *Pocahontas* would have been sentenced to a firing squad by any reasonable judge and jury. But not by doughboys. There wasn't anyone among us who would have delayed a single day, even if it meant being given the bridal suite on the world's finest luxury liner.

For the first couple of days out, the seas were fierce, making most of us desperately seasick. Our meals were served on deck where we couldn't avoid seeing the motion of the ship. We ate them all standing because, quite literally, there was no room to sit down. The unvaried menu consisted of a dipperful of slum-gullion. If the ship took a sudden roll, the contents of our mess kits—and, sometimes, of our stomachs—would land on our neighbors. At the best of times, there was no way to get to the rail when nausea struck. Latrine and bathing facilities were woefully inadequate and the whole ship soon reeked of unwashed men, vomit and other bodily functions.

All day long, we'd push each other around the deck, trying in vain for a change of scene. A few enterprising fellows tried to fish without much success. Each evening, we watched the sun sink in the west, knowing we were one day closer home.

The nights were almost unendurable. Tiers of chicken-wire bunks were installed below and we had to undergo the most back-twisting gymnastics to crawl into our places through bare inches of space. The heat from the boiler room was hellish; the steady thump of the engines and bilge pumps created a constant source of anxiety. Small wonder that, if a man did manage to fall asleep in such a hell hole, he was likely to awaken, panting in terror, sure he was back in the Argonne with shells falling around him or watching his buddy die in a machine-gun fusillade. The bugle call each morning was as welcome as Gabriel's trumpet will be.

Easter Sunday, still at sea. On the ninth day out, the 112th band played a concert from the fantail. On the morning of April 29, a wireless informed us that the vessel would dock at Philadelphia. The next morning, the rail was so crowded it's a miracle we didn't push each other overboard. When the lighthouse at Cape May, New Jersey was sighted, every man on deck cheered until he was too hoarse to continue. I was not the only man who could scarcely see for the tears in my eyes. I still remember the profound gratitude to God that I had survived to come home and an almost unbearable pain for the boys who had not.

We pulled into Delaware Bay where a veritable fleet of tugs with whistles wildly blowing, big yachts, fishing boats . . . all jammed with happy people screaming with joy, jumping up and down and waving in welcome. The *Pocahontas* was the first troopship to land at Philadelphia and the city was there in force. We hardly gave the longshoremen time to set the gangplank before our hobnailed boots were thundering down it so we could walk once more on American soil. Home. Home. Home. By God, we were home!

Everywhere we looked, Red Cross ladies, Philadelphia matrons, young ladies stood laughing, weeping, holding out big chunks of homemade cake and ice cream, candy. When we tasted these offerings of American women's hands, we knew we were home indeed. Most of us filled out the free telegraph blanks the Salvation Army supplied so we could send word to our dear ones that we were coming home. Others simply entrusted their letters and postcards to one of the kind ladies who promised to send them on their way.

We boarded the train for Fort Dix, New Jersey and arrived at nighttime. In the morning, it was back to the delousing mills where the little varmints were, at last, vanquished for good. We were supplied with clean, lice-free clothing.

On Monday, May 5, the paymaster gave us each sixty dollars and rail fare home. A few fellows stopped in Philadelphia for a bang-up celebration; most of us couldn't wait to get home.

We arrived in the most beautiful little town in the whole world— Huntingdon, Pennsylvania—before dark. Every citizen in town not too young, old or sick to walk, came to meet the train at the station. The happy din was sheer ecstasy to us. However, we couldn't yet rush into the arms of our loved ones; until we turned in our weapons, we weren't civilians.

What a glorious evening! I can see it still, dear faces in the crowd, parents, brothers, sisters, wives, sweethearts, children . . . even one baby boy named Argonne to commemorate the place where his father had fought. I can still see another young wife, too, Mabel McEwen, who, because of poor communication from the War Department, did not yet know her husband, Tom, had died at Fismes. She searched the crowd anxiously with her eyes and then began to grab at doughboys' sleeves. "Where's Tom?" she asked. "Has anyone seen Tom?"

We'd faced the worst the Hun could throw against us but no one wanted to be the one to tell Mabel and her baby daughter that Tom was not with us.

In the midst of our joy at being home, there was not a one of us who didn't silently mourn the comrades who'd gone west ahead of us. None of us had escaped without small wounds, gas inhalation or the emotional trauma they called shell-shock then. Most of us would suffer for the rest of our days with recurrent dysentery and nightmares. But the carefree boys of Company F had come home men. We'd fought the war that would end all wars. Little Argonne would never have to lie in a bloody trench.

APPENDIX A

TRANSLATION OF LETTER C. E. BAKER TOOK FROM
WALLET OF THE GERMAN SOLDIER, AUGUST 1918

Translated by George Dolnikowski
March 18, 1997

Date . . .

Biography of
one . . .

I . . . of Protestant faith, was born on April 30, 1896, in Hanover as a son of the landowner Albert Eggers. In 1899 my parents moved to North America, state of Iowa, where they took over a large successful farm. During the spring of 1914, my family returned to Hanover in Germany so that I would be able to receive better education. It is here that my father lives on his property. During Eastertime of 1914, I entered the Lister Private High School for Boys in Hanover, Schatzkamp #28. In the summer of 1915, I had to enter military training; the unit is known as the Guard Infantry. On the 3rd of November 1915, I entered the military service in the Infantry Regiment #203, stationed at Z[vaven?]. On the 21st of January 1916, I passed the exams at Konigsstadtischen Overrealschule in Berlin at Pasteurstrasse 44–46. Now I was free to enter the military service for one year. Beginning in May of 1916, I was moved to the Reserve Regiment #203, 3rd Co., station near Verdun. In June our regiment came to Russia, not far from Luzk, where I was wounded on the 23rd of June 1916 (right upper side and lower part of arm). On the 2nd of August 1916 I joined the Reserve Battalion from where I was moved to the Infantry Regiment #419 in Z[in?] on November 6, 1916. On 11th December 1916, I came to the 4th Guard Regiment, 3rd Co. in the battle area or the field position.

126

There were battles by Perrone, Ainse, Argonerwald and Reims. There were also offensives near Tarnopol [in Russia], Riga, and Cainorai-St. Quentin [near Metz]. On 4th April 1918 I was wounded for the second time near Griv[?]. It was my left hand that was wounded. Fully recovered, I was sent on the 22nd of May 1918 to a Reserve Battalion in Berlin.

In the middle of January 1917 I took part in a M.G. course and on the second of February 1917 I took a 4-week-long course for lower-ranked officers in Vengelles. On the 26th of November 1917 I was sent again to attend a course for lower-ranked officers in Vieil, St. Remy.

On 7th June 1917 I was promoted to a Pvt. 1st Class and on the 11th Nov. to a non-commissioned officer. On 4th Nov. 1917 I was decorated and received an Iron Cross 2nd Class.

Date . . .

Taking into consideration my biography, my free entrance in the military service for one year, and my blameless record, I agree after the war to remain in military service for two more years. My father agreed to pay the costs; he holds a 6th war bond in my name valued at 10,000 marks. More information about me can be readily supplied by my former school director Herr Eb? in Hanover, Sechanstrasse 30.

Respectfully,

. . . .

APPENDIX B

Roster

Company "F", 112th U.S. Infantry
Captain David Sutherland, Company Commander

1st Lieutenant Joseph P. Connell
1st Lieutenant Harry E. Robb
2nd Lieutenant William M. Corbin
2nd Lieutenant James R. Thompson
2nd Lieutenant John W. Dodge
First Sergeant Quinton J. McClelland
Mess Sergeant Frank L. Dillon
Supply Sergeant Philip E. P. Brine

Sergeants

Nicholas E. Musgrave
William E. Emery
Harry M. Myers
Harry P. Shields
James C. Richey
Frederick S. Burford

William P. LaMere
Frank R. Fleming
Walter W. Conrad
Xopher E. Moyer
Sewell E. Cutshall
Lewis H. Knode

Corporals

Robert R. Huddleson
John P. Connell
Harold P. Anderson
George B. Ross
Edward C. Gribben
Harry A. DeWoody
Harry M. Eakin
James B. Frankenberger
Frank W. Mehrten
Frank E. Hedley

Sherman A. Dunlap
Ross E. Perrine
Earl F. Rishel
Harry D. Figard
William B. Holder
James H. White
Floyd Krepps
Elmer R. Martz
Fred A. Steele
Chester E. Baker

Corporals

Cassius F. Whitehall
Edwin H. Griffith
Robert L. Jones
Charles E. Dunkle

Thomas D. McEwen
Edward B. Shoff
James E. Strange
Frank K. Myers

Cooks

George W. Young
Emil F. Mack
Clarence E. Rosenberg
Awra C. Adams

Mechanics

William E. Clark
Gilbert T. Bishop
Charles L. Gray
Horace C. Corbin

Buglers

Eric A. Vogan

Roy W. Scott

Privates

Africa, Oliver
Agnew, George
Alexander, James S.
Ambrose, William E.
Anderson, Carl W.
Anderson, Charles W.
Anderson, John
Appleby, Robert G.
Austra, Joseph E.
Bailey, Clarence L.
Bagshaw, Frank D.
Banks, Jesse P.
Barlett, Clarence E.
Baumgardner, John C.
Baumgardner, Jacob R.
Beatty, Finley
Beers, William G.
Beck, Oscar
Beck, Samuel
Berlin, Oren C.
Blair, Edward L.
Blyler, Fred
Boner, Joseph A.
Bottomfield, James S.
Bowers, LeRoy
Bowman, Jesse C.
Bradley, Bernard P.
Bradley, Luther A.

Bradley, Richard H.
Brennan, Louis J.
Brindle, Daniel
Brindle, Elmer J.
Brown, James H.
Brown, Preston G.
Brown, Richard C.
Brown, Raymond A.
Brown, William E.
Buffett, John W.
Buffett, Roland
Burke, Adam
Butler, Russell O.
Callan, John J.
Clune, James E.
Coffman, Floyd
Coffman, Carl G.
Cohen, Nathan J.
Coldren, Clyde W.
Corbin, Harry D.
Corbin, Wilbur F.
Cotterman, William A.
Cowher, Carlton M.
Cozad, Charles H.
Cramer, Homer W.
Creswell, Leroy
Cristini, Frank
Crownover, Oscar H.

Privates

Crownover, Roy S.
Davis, Harry W.
Dean, Jay V.
Decker, Charles B.
DeMart, James D.
Dilley, Norman L.
Dorworth, Harold M.
Doyle, Jonathon F.
Drolsbaugh, David B
Drolsbaugh, Fred M.
Dunkle, John A.
Duriel, Thaddeus
Earsman, Willis
Edwards, Robert H.
Edwards, James W.
Engles, William J.
English, William E.
Estep, Harry
Evans, Ralph W.
Ewing, Plum L.
Farren, John W.
Feaster, Elmer C.
Fish, Raymond W.
Flake, Fred
Fry, John M.
Gamble, George S.
Gibboney, George E.
Gibbs, Arthur E.
Godard, George F.
Goss, Harry J.
Graham, Robert B.
Greer, Jesse G.
Greggs, David
Hagans, James H.
Hall, William E.
Hamel, William
Hamman, Clarence
Hamor, Edward B.
Hardy, Gordon
Harton, Albert F.
Harvey, Frank C.
Hawkins, Oliver B.

Hays, Carl
Hawn, Chalmers J.
Heck, Charles R.
Heck, Homer O.
Heckathorn, Lee J.
Hecker, Edwin C.
Heeter, John N.
Helsel, Harold S.
Henderson, Oral S.
Henzel, Francis P.
Herriman, Thomas H.
Herring, Clair F.
Herring, David H.
Hess, William H.
Hollobaugh, Charles R.
Holt, Charles W.
Homman, Frank P.
Honstine, Robert B.
Houser, Oscar
Hovis, Norman A.
Hovis, George W.
Johnson, Fred H.
Johnson, Harry W.
Johnston, Donald S.
Jones, Owen
Kepler, Merril G.
Krepps, Frederick
Kress, August J.
Kurtz, Frank W.
Kurtz, James M.
Leeper, James R.
Leonard, William J.
Lewis, James G.
Lightner, George H.
Lister, William S.
Lukehart, Harry L.
Maier, Harry M.
Maloney, George A.
Mario, Joseph D.
Mason, James E.
Matzko, John L., Jr.
McCann, John B.

Privates

McCann, Thomas P.
McKee, Lynn H.
McConnell, Robert
Mong, Melvin M.
Moore, Howard E.
Morningstar, William B.
Mulholland, Leo B.
Miller, Orthello B.
Miller, Paul A.
Minnick, Albert
Montgomery, Harry O.
Murdock, Elmer M.
Murphy, Oliver C.
Nail, Bird
Palmer, Leo W.
Palmer, William J.
Pashley, Enil F.
Pollock Earl G.
Port, Arthur A.
Porter, Andrew J.
Porter, George V.
Porter, James H.
Porter, William R.
Ricalton, Robert F.
Ross, John D.
Rupert, John L.
Saukeld, Marward L.
Saunier, Harold P.
Seaton, Harold A.
Shaffer, Clarence M.
Shuffstall, Ralph L.
Sichi, Leopoldo

Simonson, William S.
Smith, Abe D.
Smith, Clarence E.
Smith, Fred F.
Smock, Vernie H.
Snyder, Clarence E.
Speer, James H.
Spyker, William P.
Stadler, Orville E.
Stallsmith, James E.
Steel, Earl H.
Steen, Joe
Sterrett, Lester E.
Stewart, George H.
Strouss, James R.
Sullivan, Lawrence J.
Waldo, Frank M.
Weir, James B.
Weston, Norman C.
White, Donald L.
White, Robert L.
Whitesell, Carl F.
Williams, Warren E.
Wilson, James S.
Wolcott, Walter S.
Wood, George S.
Woodworth, Ray
Zauzig, Charles J.
Zuver, Edward L.

Company "F" on the Mexican Border-1916–1917

Major George B. Corbin
Captain Charles H. Hatfield
1st Lieutenant Harry E. Robb
2nd Lieutenant William M. Corbin
1st Sergeant Harry F. Lucas
1st Duty Sergeant John K. Itinger
Mess Sergeant Charles A. Wike

Sergeants

Xopher E. Moyer
Louis H. Knode
Nicholas E. Musgrave
Luther E. Park
Thomas Eichleberger

Sewell E. Cutshall
Philip Short
Ira H. Gardner
Walter Conrad
Harry McMahan

Corporals

Earl E. Rishel
Thomas D. McEwen
Harry D. Figard
James E. Strange
Clarence E. Smith
Frank K. Myers
George A. Port

Chester E. Baker
Edward B. Shoff
William B. Holder
James E. White
Floyd Krepps
Fred A. Steele
Richard E. Swivel

Cooks

Charles E. Lightner
John D. Newingham
Thomas G. Shirm

Mechanics

Horace C. Corbin
(artificer)
Charles L. Gray
(hostler)

Buglers

James E. Wilson

Maynard Saukheld

Privates, First Class

Robert C. Appleby
William E. Ambrose
James S. Bottomfield
John C. Bumgardner
Frank D. Bagshaw
Oscar P. Beck
Preston G. Brown
Roy S. Crownover
Harry D. Corbin
Levi T. Decker
Fred J. Endres
James W. Edwards
Robert H. Edwards

George F. Godard
Clarence W. Hamman
Chalmer J. Hawn
James M. Kurtz
Orthello B. Miller
Lynn H. McKee
Earl C. Pollock
Earl H. Steele
Isaac W. Steele
William P. Spyker
James B. Weir
Clyde Weir
Charles J. Zauzig

Privates

Oliver S. Africa
Carl W. Anderson
John Anderson
William A. Bagley
Clarence L. Bailey
Jesse P. Banks
Samuel H. Beck
Leroy Bowers
Jesse C. Bowman
Daniel J. Brindle
Elmer J. Brindle
Jacob R. Bumgardner
Russell O. Butler
Clyde W. Caldren
Carl C. Coffman
Nathan M. Cohan
Wilbur F. Corbin
Carlton M. Cowher
Leroy Cresswell
Frank Cristini
Frederick M. Dean
James DeMart
David Drolsbaugh
Fred M. Drolsbaugh
William English
Harry Estep
Elmer C. Feaster
Frederick Flake
John M. Fry
George S. Gamble
Joseph L. Gates
George E. Gibboney
Clair C. Gray
Gaird C. Grove
James S. Hagem
William E. Hall
William Hamel
Edward B. Hamer
John H. Hearn
Homer D. Heck

Harold S. Helsel
Francis Hensel
Claire F. Herring
William H. Hess
James F. Hoffman
Charles W. Holt
Frank Homman
Oscar Houser
Donald Johnson
Merril C. Kepler
Frank W. Kurtz
James H. Leeper
William J. Leonard
George H. Lightner
William S. Lister
Hugh Little
Harry L. Lukehart
Harry M. Maier
Fred Maines
Bert Mains
James D. McHugh
Russell B. Means
Paul A. Miller
Albert Minnick
William Morningstar
Chester S. Peightol
William A. Pope
Thomas Price
Stanley L. Rackley
Chalmer Rittenhouse
Ralph E. Showalter
Chic Strange
Raymond F. Trimble
Charles S. Trimer
George E. Weaver
Melvin H. Wilt
Carlton C. Wike
George E. Wolfe
Paul S. Worthy
Wilbur C. Young

One by One
by C. E. Baker

One by one old soldiers die,
One by one they are no more,
And their comrades mourn their loss,
As they leave this mortal shore.

Standing by an open grave,
One more flag-draped coffin rests,
Friends and comrades gather 'round,
As they pay their last respects.

When the solemn rites are done,
And the chaplain turns away,
Mournful notes of bugle stir,
Mem'ries of a bygone day.

One by one they drop from rank,
Just as did the blue and gray,
Soldier boys in olive drab,
Destined, too, to pass away.

I look into the newest grave,
Then turn my blurred eyes to the sky,
Battalions of once-living comrades,
Seem to march in my heart's eye.

Far beyond that field of blue,
I seem to hear a martial strain,
As they march and counter-march,
Phantoms of my tired brain.

Few there are to mourn old soldiers,
Fewer still of them remain,
Who alone seem to acknowledge,
What they gave was not in vain.

I am comforted to know,
They'll never more need to be brave,
'Midst the falling shot and shell,
. . . Or standing by a comrade's grave.

INDEX

(First names are included where known.)